T0065824

WHOLESOME FEAR

WHOLESOME FEAR

Transforming Your Anxiety
about
Impermanence & Death

LAMA ZOPA RINPOCHE

AND KATHLEEN McDONALD

Wisdom Publications • Boston

Wisdom Publications
199 Elm Street
Somerville MA 02144 USA
www.wisdompubs.org

© 2010 Lama Zopa Rinpoche
All rights reserved.

No part of this book may be reproduced in any form or by any means,
electronic or mechanical, including photography, recording, or by any
information storage and retrieval system or technologies now known or
later developed, without permission in writing from the publisher.

Library of Congress Cataloging-in-Publication Data
Thubten Zopa, Rinpoche, 1945–
 Wholesome fear : transforming your anxiety about impermanence & death /
Lama Zopa Rinpoche and Kathleen McDonald.
    p. cm.
 Includes bibliographical references.
 ISBN 0-86171-630-2 (pbk. : alk. paper)
 1. Religious life—Buddhism. 2. Anxiety—Religious aspects—Buddhism. 3.
Death—Religious aspects—Buddhism. I. McDonald, Kathleen, 1952– II. Title.
 BQ4302.T53 2010
 294.3'423—dc22

                                      2009044737

14 13 12 11 10
 5 4 3 2 1

Cover photo by Josh Bartok, www.shobophoto.com. Cover design by TLJBJE.
Interior design by Tony Lulek. Set in Bembo 11.75/16. Image of Medicine
Buddha on page 124 by Robert Beer.

Wisdom Publications' books are printed on acid-free paper and meet the
guidelines for permanence and durability of the Production Guidelines for
Book Longevity of the Council on Library Resources.

Printed in the United States of America.

♻ This book was produced with environmental mindfulness. We have elected to
print this title on 30% PCW recycled paper. As a result, we have saved the following resources: 14 trees, 4 million BTUs of energy, 1,326 lbs. of greenhouse gases,
6,389 gallons of water, and 388 lbs. of solid waste. For more information, please visit
our website, www.wisdompubs.org. This paper is also FSC certified. For more information, please visit www.fscus.org.

Table of Contents

More Meditations
Kathleen McDonald

APPENDIXES: HOW TO BEGIN MEDITATING RIGHT NOW

Preface

In our busy lives, we may not give much thought to our deaths and, indeed, we may be uncomfortable even thinking about death. Perhaps we feel it is too depressing and fear that thinking about death will make us sad; or maybe we fear that thinking about death will take all the joy out of living. Yet in truth, when we actively think about death and prepare for our own deaths, the opposite actually happens: we connect more to the peace, fulfillment, and happiness available in our lives. What's more, our fear of death starts to disappear.

This book contains Lama Zopa Rinpoche's essential advice for the time of death and for finding the deepest fulfillment in life. It provides a plethora of practical advice to prepare for your own death—starting now! You will also gain knowledge of the heart practices useful at the time of death, as well as practices that can help others who are dying.

For those who would like to go further with this material, the Foundation for the Preservation of the Mahayana Tradition (FPMT) publishes an expanded version of this book under the title *Heart Advice for Death and Dying*. In addition, a companion volume called *Heart Practices for Death and Dying* offers traditional Tibetan Buddhist practices to benefit the dying and the dead. Both are available from the FPMT at www.fpmt.org/shop.

A book such as this cannot be created without the help of many people. We extend our deepest thanks to Venerable Tenzin Chogkyi for creating the original outline of the book, to the creators and editors of the Discovering Buddhism program and to the Lama Yeshe Wisdom Archive for providing source material, to Venerable Constance Miller and Sherry Tillery for their editorial feedback, and to Josh Bartok of Wisdom Publications for his work in creating this final version that you hold in your hands. We especially thank Kathleen McDonald for her beautiful teachings which provide the introduction to this work, and for her skillful presentation of the meditations at the end of the book. And from the bottom of our hearts we thank Lama Zopa Rinpoche, who, out of his great compassion and kindness, has made these essential heart instructions available for the benefit of all. We hope this book brings everlasting happiness to sentient beings everywhere.

Gyalten Mindrol
FPMT International Office
Portland, Oregon, USA

Introduction

by Kathleen McDonald

The Buddha told his listeners not to blindly believe what was written in any sacred book or spoken by any holy person, including himself. He said we should always use our own intelligence to check everything out for ourselves and determine for ourselves what is true and false, right and wrong, useful and not useful.

I am writing this introduction a few weeks after the death of my mother. Her death was a difficult experience for me—of course it's always painful losing someone you love, someone important in your life—but it was also beautiful and inspiring. My mother was diagnosed with advanced-stage cancer in early December and died at home three weeks later. I feel very fortunate that I could stay with her during those last weeks of her life, until her last breath. She was completely accepting of her illness and impending death, was not unhappy or afraid, and instead was peaceful, loving and caring toward others, and even cheerful.

I believe her life and death were an illustration of the main theme of this book: how we die depends on how we live. If we wish to be peaceful and positive at the time of death, we need to develop and live those qualities as much as we can in our life. My mother's ability to be serene, content, and positive as she neared death was the result of a life of faith, gratitude, optimism, goodness, and kindness to others.

The subject of death makes a lot of people uneasy. We as a culture don't like to talk, hear, or even think about death. If something related to death comes up in a conversation, there is an often uncomfortable silence—and then, more often than not, we quickly change the subject. Part of our anxiety is because we just don't know much about death, what to do about it, how to prepare for it. We don't have courses on "Death Management" at our local community college or adult-education center. This problem has been somewhat remedied over the last forty years or so, thanks to the hospice movement and writers such as Elisabeth Kübler-Ross and Stephen Levine. Death and dying have come out of the shadows, as it were, and are now more acceptable topics of conversation—but there is still a long way to go.

Death is a very important subject in Buddhism. There is a great deal of information on what death is all about, why it happens, how we can prepare for our own death, and how we can help others who are dying. In this book, Lama Zopa Rinpoche shares with us the wisdom of the Tibetan Buddhist tradition on this subject. Some readers may not be familiar with Buddhism, and particularly Tibetan Buddhism, so in this introduction I will explain some basic Buddhist ideas about life, death, and what happens after death.

The Buddhist World View

There are different ideas about where we come from, why we are here, and what happens to us when we die. Some people believe in a creator who gave us life, intelligence, free will, and a soul that will live forever after death. Other people believe that we are nothing more than a collection of biological substances and processes, and that our life simply ceases when we die, like a flame going out.

The Buddhist explanation is that we are part of a universe in which there are myriad worlds and living beings, continuously coming into existence and going out of existence. This situation is known as *samsara*, or cyclic existence. There is no beginning to this process and no creator. The driving force behind everything that happens—in the universe as well as in our individual lives—is *karma*, the law of cause and effect. More will be said about this later, but in brief, karma means that we experience the results or effects of our actions. It means that in an important way we are the creators of our own experiences.

Cyclic existence is not a perfect, delightful situation, but rather an imperfect, unsatisfactory one. We are born, age, and die—again and again, across moments and across universal spans of time. Between each birth and death, we experience many difficulties: sickness, loss, relationship problems, disappointment, depression, irritation, worries, and all the rest. Of course, not all of our experiences are bad—we have pleasant ones as well, but even those are unsatisfying: they don't completely free us from our problems, and they don't ever last.

This may sound depressing, and in fact Buddhism is often misinterpreted as being pessimistic, but the Buddha did not teach only about problems and suffering; he also explained that there is an alternative to samsara: *nirvana*, or liberation, the state of perfect peace, bliss, and freedom from all problems. Moreover, there is the state of complete enlightenment, or buddhahood, the attainment of which enables us to be of benefit to all beings everywhere. These states are attainable by each and every one of us. In fact, according to Buddhism, that is the ultimate purpose of our life: striving to attain either nirvana—self-liberation from the cycle of birth and death—or enlightenment, in order to help all beings become free. But we don't have to wait until reaching nirvana or enlightenment for things to improve. In fact, as we progress any distance along the spiritual path, we will experience less suffering and more happiness, and our ability to benefit others will likewise increase.

The Buddha told his listeners not to blindly believe what was written in any sacred book or spoken by any holy person, including himself. He said we should always use our own intelligence to check everything out for ourselves and determine for ourselves what is true and false, right and wrong, useful and not useful. And indeed we *can* know these things for ourselves. Our minds have unlimited potential; the very nature of the mind is clear, pure, and endowed with many positive qualities. This clarity and purity is only temporarily clouded by obstructing factors such as our delusions, our grasping, our fear, as well as past karma—the very things that keep us stuck in samsara. These factors can be purified gradually through spiritual practice, so that the pure, clear "buddha-nature" of our minds can become manifest.

The attainment of enlightenment does not happen instantly. It happens gradually over time, as we engage in spiritual practice, step by step on the spiritual path. And one of the first steps in this process is acknowledging the reality of impermanence of all things, including ourselves and those we love. And this means deeply acknowledging the reality of death.

The Importance of Remembering Impermanence and Death

The Buddha frequently spoke about impermanence: that things are not fixed and static, but transitory, changing moment by moment by moment. This is true of people and other living beings, everything in nature, and all creations. Nothing will last forever; everything will inevitably die or pass away.

The Buddha said:

> All collections end up running out,
> The high end up falling,
> Meeting ends in separation,
> Living ends in death.

The Buddha also recommended that we *accept*, *contemplate*, and *remain aware* of impermanence and death, rather than denying or avoiding this reality. He said:

> Of all ploughing, ploughing in the autumn is supreme.
> Of all footprints, the elephant's is supreme.
> Of all perceptions, remembering death and impermanence
> is supreme.

Without remembering death and impermanence, we may imagine we will live forever; we may imagine we don't have to prepare for death. Or we may think that the only purpose in life is to enjoy ourselves as much as possible. Then, with such attitudes, we may become careless about what we do and fail to do what is really important with our life. Unmindful of death, we may act in ways that are selfish, dishonest, or even cruel—harming both others and ourselves. And then in the end, if we live in such a way, we may die with regret and fear.

On the other hand, awareness of the transitory nature of everything leads us to be careful about what we do, and stimulates positive attitudes and behavior. People who have near-death experiences confirm this. These are people who have a close encounter with death, but then have a second chance at life. They come back with a strong sense of the importance of being loving and caring toward others, of the insignificance of materialistic pursuits, and of the crucial importance of having a spiritual dimension in their life.

Fortunately, we don't have to have a near-death experience to realize these important truths; being consistently mindful of impermanence and death will have the same wholesome effect.

Death Is Not the End of Everything

According to Buddhism, our present life is just one in a series of lives that stretch far back into the beginningless past, and will continue far into the endless future, until we attain liberation or enlightenment.

A person is a combination of body and mind. The body consists of all the physical aspects of our being: skin, bones, blood, organs, cells, atoms, and so forth. The mind, on the other hand, is non-physical; it is not made of atoms, cells, or any material substance. The mind consists of all of our conscious experiences: thoughts, emotions, perceptions, memories, dreams, fantasies, and so on. Yet it is not a fixed, static phenomenon, but an ever-changing stream flowing moment-to-moment with experiences. One moment there's a happy thought or feeling, the next moment an unhappy one. We are loving at one moment, angry at another. Memories of the past and fantasies of the future flow in and out amid perceptions of the present moment. The mind, like a river, is never the same from one moment to the next.

While we are alive, our body and mind have an interdependent relationship: what happens in our minds affects our bodies; what happens in our bodies affects our minds. Even so, the mind-body relationship is transient and ends with death. Death is the point at which the mind separates from the body. Death is not a final end, but rather a gateway to another life. However, what passes from this life to the next is not a fixed, personal identity or soul, but rather the impersonal, ever-changing mind-stream, carrying with it imprints of all we have done in our life: seeds planted in the past that will grow and come to fruition in the future. These imprints determine our future experiences.

Karma

Karma is a Sanskrit word that literally means "action." Each time we do an action, an "imprint" is left on our minds that will bring results in the future when the right conditions come together.

Karma can be divided into actions of body, speech, and mind. We create karma with our physical actions, our words, and even with our thoughts. Also, in a general way, karma can be divided into positive and negative, or wholesome and unwholesome. The main factor that determines whether an action of body, speech, or mind is wholesome or unwholesome is the motivation behind it. We create positive karma when we act with the wish to help and not harm others, and when we act with our minds free of delusions such as anger and attachment. The future results of such actions will also be positive, will also be wholesome. On the other hand, when we are motivated by a negative attitude such as anger or attachment, and do actions such as hurting someone, stealing, or being dishonest, we create negative karma. Negative karma will always give rise to unpleasant experiences.

Lama Zopa Rinpoche's teacher, Lama Thubten Yeshe, used to say that we don't have to wait until our next life to observe how karma works. Even in this life, in this one day, we can see that our attitudes and behavior at one point in time affect our experiences at a later point; if we look closely, we can see how our past affects us even now.

Karma is not something fixed, like words carved in stone; just because we have done something negative doesn't mean we will necessarily have to suffer. We can *purify* our negative karma and not have to experience its suffering results. Karmic purification is a psychological process involving four steps:

(1) Feeling regret for what we have done;
(2) Relying upon helpful objects of refuge, such as the

Buddha or another higher power who is wise, compassionate, and forgiving, as well as on cultivating positive attitudes such as love and compassion;

(3) Doing something positive as a remedy to the negative action;

(4) Resolving to refrain from repeating the action in the future.

There is no karma that cannot be purified by using these four steps.

Understanding and appreciating the reality of karma means taking responsibility. We realize that we are the creators of our experiences. We can't blame anyone for our problems, and we can't expect that someone else can make us happy. This understanding is crucial for our present life: if we want happiness and positive experiences, we must create the right causes; and if we don't want unhappiness and bad experiences, we must likewise avoid creating their causes even now.

Understanding karma is also essential when we look ahead to the end of our life and after. The very experiences we will have *as we are dying* and those afterward are determined by our actions in this life. A positive, loving life leads to good experiences at death, while a selfish, destructive life leads to negative experiences at death. And the same is also true for each rebirth: wholesome karma leads to positive rebirths, and unwholesome karma to painful ones.

Aside from karma, another crucial factor that determines our experiences in rebirth is the state of mind we have at death. The reason for this is that most of us will arrive at the end of our lives with a vast collection of both positive and negative karma. Which of these karmic imprints will be the cause of our next life? That is determined by our state of mind as we die. A positive state of mind—accepting, calm, and loving—will activate one of our positive karmic imprints and propel us to a fortunate rebirth. A negative state of mind—non-accepting, clinging to people or possessions, or angry at what is happening to us—will activate one of our negative karmic imprints, propelling our minds to unfortunate rebirths.

From the Buddhist point of view, this is the main reason for aspiring to die with a positive state of mind.

The Precious Human Life

According to Buddhism, of all places of rebirth, the best from the point of view of spiritual practice is the human realm. The reason for this is that as human beings we have just the right amount of difficulties to be able to recognize the unsatisfactory situation we are in as unenlightened beings and to aspire to be free from it, but we are not so overwhelmed by problems that we are unable to do anything constructive. Most of the beings in the other realms either have too much suffering or too much pleasure to be able to develop these attitudes. This alone can give us cause for gratitude.

But even in the human realm, not everyone is in the best situation for spiritual practice, so Buddhism speaks of the "precious human rebirth." This is a particular kind of human life in which we have all the ideal internal and external conditions in which to follow a spiritual path that leads out of suffering and dissatisfaction, to genuine peace, happiness, and enlightenment. These conditions include having access to spiritual teachers and to teachings that show the path to enlightenment, having sufficient faith in these teachings, wanting to learn and practice them, and being supported in our practice by other caring people.

A precious human rebirth does not come about by chance; it is the result of creating certain causes. The main cause of such a life is living ethically, which means refraining from harmful actions such as killing, stealing, lying, and other such clear ways of causing harm. Other important causes are generosity, patience, being energetic about doing wholesome actions, and making prayers for such a rebirth. We have such a birth now, and that means that if we have a precious human rebirth now, we must have created these causes in our past lives. And if we want such a rebirth next time, we need to create these causes now, in this life.

The usual way in which the precious human rebirth is discussed in the Buddhist teachings is in terms of recognizing that we are extremely fortunate to have such a life. This is because of the many meaningful and beneficial things we can do with this life, for ourselves and others, now and in the future. The precious human rebirth is rare and difficult to obtain, so while we have this opportunity, before it ends, we need to use it wisely and carefully.

Bodhichitta—the Aspiration to Attain Enlightenment

Enlightenment is a state we can all attain—but we first need to develop *bodhichitta*, the aspiration to attain enlightenment in order to help all beings. With this motivation, everything we do—even ordinary actions like eating, sleeping, and working—becomes a cause for enlightenment. Lama Zopa Rinpoche says that the best attitude we can have as we die is also that of bodhichitta. Therefore, generating bodhichitta and directing our energy toward enlightenment is the best way to use our human life and our death as well.

But this does not mean that we cannot help others until we are enlightened. Generating and practicing bodhichitta also means doing whatever we can to help others *now*, and when we do, bodhichitta adds another dimension to such actions. For example, when we give food to a homeless person or help our neighbor carry her groceries, if our long-term motivation is attaining enlightenment so that we can help all beings become free of all their suffering and attain the perfect state of enlightenment as well, then these simple actions bring us closer to enlightenment, and will ultimately become beneficial for all beings.

Doing activities with bodhichitta can simply mean being as kind as possible, with mindful awareness trying to help others and avoid harming them, and learning to be less selfish and more altruistic.

It is possible for all of us to develop full-fledged bodhichitta in this life and indeed there are various methods for doing so. These methods involve meditating on and making our minds familiar with certain wholesome thoughts and attitudes. The more our minds become familiar with these, the more bodhichitta will arise naturally and effortlessly.

One method is known as "equalizing and exchanging oneself with others" and involves contemplating five points:

The equality of oneself and others. All beings—I and everyone else—are equal in wanting to be happy and wanting to not suffer. There is no reason why my wish to be happy and free of suffering is more important than anyone else's.

The faults of self-cherishing. The self-cherishing attitude (selfishness)—caring more for myself than for others—is the cause of problems, and is an obstacle to real peace and happiness.

The benefits of cherishing others. Unselfishness—cherishing others more than myself—is the cause of all happiness and peace up to enlightenment.

Exchanging oneself with others. By contemplating the faults of self-cherishing and the benefits of cherishing others, I realize that it's better to be less concerned with myself and more caring toward others. Therefore, I resolve to work on changing my attitude from self-cherishing to cherishing others.

The practice of "taking and giving" (tonglen). This is a power-ful meditation for transforming the mind from self-cherishing to cherishing others. Tonglen involves two steps: first, you meditate on compassion, the wish for others to be free from suffering, and then imagine *taking* their suffering into yourself, using it to annihilate the self-cherishing attitude. Second, you meditate on love, the wish for others to be happy, and imagine *giving* all your happiness, good qualities, and positive karma to others, making them happy. Lama Zopa Rinpoche presents a meditation on tonglen in section IV.

Fear as a Motivator

In this book, Lama Zopa Rinpoche discusses how fear of death can be transformed in a skillful and wholesome way to have a more peaceful, meaningful life, and to be better prepared for death when it happens. Some people have no difficulty recognizing and acknowledging that they are afraid of or anxious about death—which means they are not in denial over the universal fact of impermanence—but they may nonetheless have the problem of being *so* afraid or *so* anxious that they become paralyzed whenever they think of it, and then push it out of awareness. If we feel this way, we will never get the opportunity to face these fears and learn how to manage them. And if we don't, when death does inevitably happen, or even when we learn that sometime soon it might, we panic, overwhelmed by fears. Fortunately, we can learn to deal with fear and even overcome it, and as a result we will be able to face death calmly, with acceptance.

There are other people who may think they have no fear of death. Some of these people are being honest, but some are in denial. I know, because I used to be like that. When I was in my teens I had a kind of flippant attitude about death, thinking, "Oh well, if it happens, it's okay. Whatever. I'm not afraid." That attitude changed when I attended my first meditation course in 1974 at Kopan Monastery in Nepal. I had heard teachings on death and the importance of meditating on death, but I did not take them very seriously. One night during the course, there was an earthquake as we sat meditating with Lama Zopa Rinpoche. It was not very strong, but we could hear the voices of people in the nearby villages, crying out in fear, and Rinpoche suddenly said in a serious voice, "Meditate on bodhichitta." My immediate thought was "We're going to die!" and my mind, instead of meditating on bodhichitta, went into total panic. I've never felt such fear in my life—and because we were sitting in meditation (or trying to, anyway) the contents of my mind were especially vivid to me, like a movie on a big screen. I was frozen with fear, unable to think of anything positive, anything helpful.

After a few moments (which seemed like ages) the earth stopped shaking, the people stopped screaming, everything again became calm, and I thought, "Whew! We're not going to die. Thank goodness!" That experience was immensely valuable because I realized just how fragile life is, and how it can be lost in a moment. More importantly perhaps, I also realized that I was in fact afraid of dying and completely unprepared for death. And I felt certain that when death did happen, I did not want to die in such a state of panic. I wanted to have a peaceful, positive state of mind. So that experience gave me a lot of energy to work on my mind, to learn how to keep it peaceful and positive. Now, when I hear people say "I'm not afraid of death" or "Death is no big deal, we don't need to talk about it or meditate on it," I wonder how well they know their own minds.

All of us need to check our minds carefully and—above all— *honestly* to see whether or not we are afraid of death. How do you feel when you are almost in a car accident? What is your reaction when a friend or relative is diagnosed with a terminal illness or when you attend a funeral? In such situations, is your mind calm and relaxed or is there tension, stress, and fear? Are there knots in your stomach? If there is fear of death in your mind and you deny that fear, you will probably have difficulty later, at the time of death. But, if you can acknowledge the fear now and learn to deal with it, you are better prepared to face death calmly.

How can we deal with fear? A general method is simply to look into the fear and try to understand what it's all about. What exactly are you afraid of? And once you figure that out, ask yourself: is there anything I can do? If there is something that can be done, do it!

For example, you may be afraid of pain. This fear is to some extent unnecessary because not everyone has pain when they die, and for those who do have pain, medication is usually available. If you don't like the idea of medication, you can learn methods such as meditation for dealing with pain. If you are afraid of separating from your loved ones and possessions, you can start to work on overcoming attachment (there are many methods in Buddhism that help you to do that). When I examine my own fear of death, I find that it's not so much death that I am afraid of, but my *reaction* to death. I'm afraid of being overwhelmed by disturbing emotions, and unable to stay calm and clear-minded. So, to counteract that, I am learning how to deal with my mind, how to keep it positive and free of disturbing thoughts.

That is what Lama Zopa Rinpoche is saying when he speaks of having a *wholesome* fear of death. He is saying that if we never think about death and always avoid the subject, we will not recognize our fear of death. And if we don't recognize that fear, we will not do what we need to in order to be free of fear, and then we won't be prepared for death. Thus a certain amount of fear of death is appropriate and even, in a way, *wholesome* in that it encourages us to really work with the true source of our fear.

What we should fear is not death, but dying with an *uncontrolled mind*, and dying without having done anything positive in our life.

And the way to avoid such a death is to train in spiritual practice—Dharma—during our life. Therefore, remembering death, especially the fact that it could happen any moment, is a powerful incentive to engage in spiritual practice.

You may ask, isn't fear inherently or necessarily *negative*? It all depends on what we are afraid of, on whether the danger is real or imaginary, and on how we deal with and respond to our fear. If there is a real danger, and we deal wisely with our fear, it will motivate us to avoid or somehow address what we are afraid of. For example, fear of being in a car accident motivates us to drive safely. Fear of sickness motivates us to eat well and follow a healthy lifestyle. Fear of the painful consequences of negative actions motivates us to avoid them and to do positive actions instead. Fear of an uncontrolled mind at the time of death motivates us to learn how to keep our minds positive, free of disturbing, negative thoughts. These are constructive ways of working with fears that are realistic. On the other hand, fear can be negative if it is imaginary or exaggerated, or if we do not deal with it wisely but let ourselves be overwhelmed or immobilized.

From a Buddhist perspective, the reason that we have fear is because we have ignorance that sees everything—our self, others, and all things—in an incorrect way. Ignorance is the basis for other delusions such as attachment, wishing never to separate from loved ones and cherished possessions, and aversion, wanting to be distant from unpleasant people and experiences. Any time we examine one of our fears, we will most probably find one or both of these delusions behind it. So from this point of view, we can say that fear *is* negative and something to be overcome. One of the qualities of a Buddha, an enlightened being, is freedom from all fears. But until we reach the state where we are free from fear, it is best to acknowledge and work wisely with our fears.

Meditation

The subject of meditation is vast, far beyond the scope of this book, but a few words here might be helpful to readers who have little experience of it.

In general, the purpose of practicing meditation is to transform the mind from negative to positive. The word for meditation in Tibetan, *gom*, literally means "to be familiar." Meditation involves making our minds familiar with positive attitudes such as love, compassion, and wisdom, and "de-familiarizing" ourselves with negative ones such as anger, attachment, and ignorance. By practicing meditation regularly over a period of time, we will have fewer negative thoughts arising in our minds, and more positive ones.

There are many different kinds of meditation, but they can all be included in two categories: concentration meditation and analytical meditation. Concentration meditation involves focusing the mind on just one object, such as the breath or an image of the Buddha, without thinking about the object or anything else. In order to succeed in this practice we must learn to stop the "chattering" mind, and to cultivate a silent, still, clear state of mind. The purpose of this form of meditation is developing single-pointed concentration, an essential tool for traversing the spiritual path.

Analytical meditation, on the other hand, involves thinking and analyzing. It is used to recognize mistaken concepts and attitudes that we have—those that cause suffering to ourselves and others—and to familiarize ourselves with correct and beneficial ones. The ultimate purpose of this kind of meditation is to develop the wisdom that sees the true nature of things.

Most of the meditations included in this book are of the analytical variety. If you wish to practice them, sit in a place that is as quiet and free of distractions as possible. It's good if you can sit cross-legged, but that's not essential; it's perfectly okay to meditate sitting in a chair.

Whichever way you sit, keep your back straight; this enables your mind to be more clear and focused.

Begin the meditation with a few minutes of stilling your mind, letting go of all other thoughts and concerns. Focusing on and counting your breath can help you to do this. Once your mind is calm, generate a positive motivation for doing the meditation, for example, "I wish to practice meditation in order to decrease the negative energy in my mind and to increase my positive qualities such as love, compassion, patience, and wisdom. In this way, I will have more beneficial, positive energy to bring into my interactions with others, and to send out into the world." Or, if you are comfortable with the idea of bodhichitta, you can think, "I am going to do this meditation in order to attain enlightenment so that I can help all beings attain that state as well."

Then begin the actual meditation. If you do not know the points of the meditation from memory, you can have the book open in front of you. Read a portion of the meditation, then close your eyes and contemplate it. Feel free to bring your own ideas and experiences into your contemplation. The point is, as much as possible, to generate an actual experience of what you are meditating on. For example, the purpose of doing the nine-point meditation on death is to realize that *you are definitely going to die, that it could happen at any moment, and that you must do some spiritual practice in order to be prepared for death and what happens afterward.* The practice is to see and recognize these truths clearly. These realizations will have a powerful impact on the way you see yourself and your life, and on the way that you live your life.

However, don't expect to have such life-changing experiences right from the beginning of your practice of meditation. It takes time to learn basic skills like sitting still, keeping your mind on the meditation-object instead of wandering away, and dealing with doubts and questions that might come up in your mind during the meditation.

Meditation is not easy, and analytical meditation can be particularly tricky. It is ideal if you have access to an experienced meditator who can help you deal with whatever difficulties you encounter in your practice. Otherwise, trying to practice on your own without guidance could result in problems.

At any rate, if you do reach a point in your meditation where you have a strong experience of something such as the need to engage in spiritual practice in preparation for death, then it is best to stop the thinking and analyzing process and focus your mind on that experience as long as possible, even for just a few seconds. When the experience fades, you can return to the analytical process, or conclude the meditation. This method of combining analytical and placement/concentration meditation is how we actually bring about a transformation of our minds.

There is no fixed rule about the length of a meditation session. Initially, you could try meditating for fifteen to twenty minutes, but more or less is also okay. You can experiment with varying lengths of time to see what works best for you, according to your ability and schedule. Lama Yeshe used to say that even five minutes of meditation can be very beneficial. Quality is more important than quantity. A short session in which your mind is very focused, for example, is more worthwhile than a long session where your mind is all over the place.

When it is time to end your meditation session, make a positive conclusion to what you have thought about and experienced. For example, you might resolve to work on particular habits or attitudes you recognize as potentially disturbing to your mind at the time of death.

Finally, remember the motivation you started with and dedicate the positive energy you created during the meditation to that same purpose.

Wholesome Fear

SECTION 1

Impermanence and Death

Meditation is a force to stop problems, not something that you can only practice very quietly somewhere on a mountain. Meditations on death are meant to solve problems—but if you don't use them for their intended purpose, what's the point?

The Truth of Impermanence

Life is so fragile. Its nature is transitory. Life changes so much in a year, a month, a week, a day, an hour, a minute, and second by second. It's said that in the time it takes to snap your fingers, there are *sixty-five* distinct moments—and even in those split seconds, life changes.

You might dismissively think: "Why should I be surprised that life changes so much? Who cares that I age with each instant? That is natural; let it happen!" To think in this way is foolish—it neglects that every passing moment brings us closer to old age and death. Or, you may think, "That's true I become older—so what!" Many people try to deny the impermanent nature of their lives; they do not want to see the true nature of it at all. They try to disguise their appearance in the eyes of others, who also play the same game. No artificial effort can change eighty years into sixteen. This is an absolutely vain attempt, a waste of this precious human rebirth, a waste of the opportunity to become truly awakened, enlightened in the service of all. What's more, the enlightened mind fully realizes that the nature of the samsaric body is impermanent—subject to aging and death—and therefore is in the nature of suffering.

People who turn away from this truth labor under a double illusion: a mistaken belief that there exists some intervention that can free them from ruin and decay, and a wrong conception that a permanent self exists. Both of these are a denial of impermanence. These errors cause countless problems to arise continually and lead people to become ever more ignorant, lazy, and careless.

When we do look at the reality of impermanence, we see there are two levels of impermanence: the gross and the subtle. The gross level refers to changes of matter that happen over long periods of time; the subtle refers to inner changes of mind and invisible changes of matter that happen in the shortest part of a second.

Our minds and our senses can't perceive subtle moment-to-moment changes of matter; we can see only the gross changes from day to day and hour to hour, such as physical decay and dissolution. The great meditator Gampopa said: "This vessel-like world that existed at an earlier moment does not do so at a later one. That it seems to continue in the same way is because something else similar arises, like the stream of a waterfall."

Why should we worry about the changes of becoming old? Because as years, months, days, and split seconds are passing and we grow older, the perfect chance of attaining enlightenment given by this human rebirth is ending and I am becoming closer to death. I have the right equipment to make the trip to the Other Shore of enlightenment, and I have a pilot, a vehicle, and enough fuel—but here I sit, engine running, burning up fuel while my mind is distracted by other things. The longer my mind remains distracted, the more I miss the chance of reaching enlightenment. As the fuel burns, time grows shorter. This is the tragedy of wasting this precious human rebirth.

It is certain that you are not going to live much over one hundred years; you probably won't live past ninety. Yet even if you are going to live a million years, your life starts to finish at the time of your conception. As soon as it begins, your life starts becoming shorter. Nothing lasts; nothing remains the same.

As the seconds pass, so do the minutes made up by them. As the minutes pass, so do the hours—and months, days, years, and decades.

No matter whether your lifespan is a hundred years or a hundred thousand, you are growing older and decaying, even now—from the time your mind enters your mother's womb. Even now, you draw closer to death. And eventually you will reach the very time of your own death.

As many years as you have lived so far, that much of your life has gone; you are that much closer to death and your time to live is that much less. No matter whether you think you are young or old, whatever your age, that much of your life has finished. It is gone forever, irretrievable. And as likely as not what life you have left is shorter than that which has passed—and if it's not, it will be soon.

The Advantages of Remembering Death

We should always remember death. If we do, our minds will remain aware of the changes constantly happening within us, of how short the human life is, of how life is becoming shorter every moment. This has great benefit.

Many great yogis started by meditating on the shortness of the human life, on impermanence, and on death. Their enlightenment, their realizations, and their Dharma practice itself all came from this meditation. Their strength and ability to live an ascetic life in extremely isolated places, to practice the vast and profound subjects and attain the higher paths, to generate the incredible energy required to persevere in their practice—all these things came from reflecting deeply on the shortness of the human life, on impermanence, on death. The fact that they attained enlightenment in that lifetime was due to this very remembrance.

It takes a great deal of energy to reach enlightenment; yet the more urgently you want enlightenment, the more energy you will have to attain it. You need great energy to overcome the difficulties of practicing Dharma and following the path. Where does such energy come from? It comes from remembering the impermanence of life and death. Even the continual benefit that enlightened beings bring to all beings can be traced back to this meditation on death.

Remembering impermanence and death is also important if you just want to free yourself from samsara. Remembering impermanence and death helps put an end to all 84,000 delusions. All the different negative mind-states—the great root of ignorance, hatred, all the other wrong conceptions, all the obscurations that prevent liberation from samsara and enlightenment—can be terminated by the energy generated through remembering impermanence and death. This meditation is the original cause of the cessation of all these delusions. It is very powerful.

If you remember impermanence and death, you can also prevent the arising of temporal negative minds such as greed, ignorance, hatred, pride, jealousy, and so forth—the minds that cause you so much discomfort, suffering, and confusion. You prevent them from arising because remembering impermanence and death makes you wholesomely fear death and the shortness of the human life. Wholesome fear is a kind of fear that is very useful in making your mind peaceful, even in the present.

Not only is remembering impermanence and death useful at the beginning of practice—when it persuades you to seek out the Dharma and begin to practice instead of following your negative mind—it is also beneficial during the practice of the Dharma. Once you are on the path, it inspires you to continue your practice. Even though you are following the path, remembering death keeps you from losing track of your realizations and it helps you continue ever onward to the higher reaches of the path. Thus, remembering impermanence and death is also useful at the end of your practice.

Finally, at the time of death, this remembrance is useful because it allows you to die peacefully, with happiness, a relaxed mind, and no worries at all. This remembrance allows you to die with great joy. The person who has spent his or her life wholesomely remembering death every day, continuously purifying, creating merit, and creating as little negative karma as possible has no trouble at the time of death.

Death and Dharma

Ordinary people are usually afraid at the time of death, but for the purest Dharma practitioners, death is like returning home. True Dharma practitioners are happy and worry-free at the time of death. Even if they have not yet attained enlightenment, if they have diligently practiced the Dharma and created much merit during their life, they are also not upset at the time of death; they can die without regret. Because they have done much purification and created much merit, much good in the world, they are not afraid at the time of death.

Therefore, since there are so many benefits in remembering death, instead of being shocked or put off by all this talk about it, instead of forgetting about it or pushing thoughts of it away, you should always remember and meditate on the impermanence of life. But why does this topic shock people? Why are people put off when they are asked their age and the person replies, "Oh, you are so old!"? Because it is opposite to the way they *want* to feel, opposite to their wrong conceptions, to what they mistakenly believe. But these are all delusions; these things are the sources of so much suffering.

People always want to look young, not to age, not to change, but no matter how strongly they desire such things or how much they fight it, they have no choice: they change. No matter how much you don't want it to happen, you can't stop change; you can't stop the natural evolution of this impermanent life. No wish, no strategy, no product, no procedure, no belief can ever prevent decay; nothing can ever stop death. Even if you spend your whole life trying to look young on the outside, you still age and die. You can't stop death by forgetting about it, by never thinking about it, by closing your ears and not listening if somebody else is talking about it, by not reading about it. Nothing can stop death.

Carefully painting the outside of a piece of fruit might temporarily cause it to look beautiful and fresh, but inside it decays, loses its taste, shrivels up, and sours.

All external manipulations don't help. And trying to forget these things is not the solution. After all, if someone is coming to kill you, it doesn't help to pretend that it is not happening. Ignoring the truth doesn't avert the danger. You have to do something else.

Therefore, instead of being shocked and trying to escape from the natural way things are, do the opposite—constantly bring impermanence and death to mind. This is much more useful than trying to stop the fear that normally arises from remembering death by ignoring it, and it has so many advantages.

As the great Tibetan yogi Milarepa said, "I fled to the mountains through fear of death, and once there, I realized the absolute true nature of mind. Now, even if death comes to me, I won't be afraid."

This is very tasty, very effective.

Milarepa spent a long time naked, doing austere practices, leading an ascetic life in the mountains. It's said that his body was green, scrawny, and ugly. If he showed up in the West today, he would likely be arrested or at least shunned by society; everybody would hate the way he looked. People would want him to be hidden away out of sight.

Milarepa remembered death and felt afraid, and his fear drove him to the mountains, where he realized the absolute true nature, the reality of the mind, and thus overcame his fear of death. We should learn from his example and practice in the same way—remember death and overcome fear of it before it comes. This is the wise approach; this is wise work, the skillful method.

Another great Tibetan yogi said, "When the impermanence of life manifests to me, I won't be afraid. I can be a monk in the morning and take the body of a deity the same afternoon." Not only was he unafraid of death, but he also had the power to take a pure body, leaving his ordinary one.

By remembering death, you stop following your negative mind and therefore create less negative, unwholesome karma. The more you remember death, the better the results you experience.

Remembering death is very helpful.

The Disadvantages of
Not Remembering Death

Constantly remembering death is the only method that can fully eliminate the fear of death. If you don't remember death, you are not wholesomely afraid of it. If you are not wholesomely afraid of death, you become strongly attached to the comfort of this life and you spend your time seeking only that comfort. You do one thing for comfort, then another, then something else, and this is how your entire life goes by, continually serving attachment, serving the thought that is attached to the comfort of this life. Following this dark path, you end your life with great suffering at the time of death—for not only have you used your whole life to create the cause of suffering, you also have no happiness or peace of mind when you die.

If you don't remember death, you are controlled by attachment and follow your negative mind, saying, "Oh, I can practice Dharma in a couple of years; there is no hurry. Maybe I'll get to it in a year, in a few months' time." You put it off. Then when the time comes nearer, you again say, "Maybe next month, next year." Even though you think of the Dharma, you postpone your practice in this way. This comes from not remembering impermanence and death strongly or frequently enough. What's more, if you don't remember death, even when you do practice the Dharma, that practice isn't pure and won't lead to complete liberation, because you have made your Dharma practice serve attachment as well. Denying death—

even just subtly believing, "I am not going to die *today*"—is the worst hindrance to making your Dharma practice pure.

Because of the continual feeling "I am not going to die today," we are controlled by attachment to the comfort of this life and therefore, work only for this life. And in this way, everything we do becomes the cause of suffering. What's more, we rob ourselves of the strong motivation toward enlightenment that comes from recognizing the comfort of this life is like used toilet paper, something only to be cast aside.

If you don't have the strong motivation of wanting to achieve the supreme happiness of enlightenment, the cessation of samsara, or the happiness of future lives, and complete detachment from the comfort of this life, if the intuitive thought "I am not going to die today" constantly arises, your practice becomes impure.

The disadvantages of denying death and the advantages of continually remembering it are important to know. Remembering impermanence and death, you will have the energy and willingness to meditate on impermanence and death. And this in turn will lead to true happiness.

Meditating on Impermanence

Relating what you see in the outside world to yourself is extremely useful; indeed, it can be a type of analytical meditation. Thus:

> When you look at a river, think that just as the river flows, life finishes just as quickly.

> As the sun rises and sets, reflect that life passes just as quickly.

> As the oil in a burning lamp is steadily consumed, so too is your life.

> As the seasons pass, so does your life; as summer, autumn, winter, and spring pass quickly by, so does your life, becoming shorter and shorter, finishing more and more quickly.

While you see external things clearly changing—such as incense or candles burning down—you don't see your life finishing in the same way. Try to pay attention to what is happening around you, to the impermanence you can see everywhere. When you do, you will easily be able to understand that your life is finishing without a moment's delay.

This kind of practice is useful because it prevents your mind from becoming deluded; it makes your mind aware of change, of life becoming shorter, of the brevity of human life, of this precious human life.

So often we see external things going by quickly but never reflect on our own life. We remain totally unaware of the way in which our life is actually evolving: finishing quickly every moment. The same evolutionary changes we see outside of ourselves are happening within; this is the actual evolution of all phenomena, but we don't recognize it.

And not realizing how quickly and relentlessly life is finishing becomes the greatest hindrance to making our whole life pure. Even though we might know all about meditation or be great Dharma scholars, if we remain unaware of the actual evolution of life, we have no real wisdom; and without any real wisdom, real insight into impermanence, we won't change our lives.

If your house is susceptible to damage by flood, it is wise to check beforehand how great the danger is. If you find the danger is real, you feel wholesomely afraid and because of that fear, you make arrangements to protect your house, family, and property from being ruined by floodwaters. Then when you know you are safe, your life becomes peaceful; you have no worries. In the same way, it is necessary to make arrangements to protect your peace of mind before the flood of death arrives. Before death arrives, research the danger and act accordingly.

If you don't fear danger, you'll never make the necessary arrangements to protect yourself.

But being worried and afraid *at the time of death* doesn't help because at that point there is nothing we can do. No matter how great our suffering at the time of death, how great our fear and worry as we are dying, there is nothing then we can do. Whatever negative karma we have created, whatever the huge amount of garbage in our minds, we have to carry it all. Since we have created the cause, we have to suffer each result. It doesn't help at all because there is no time to practice. Our time is up, finished, gone.

Please remember this. And remembering death right now, do what is necessary right now to protect yourself. Practice Dharma right now, without delay.

SECTION 2

Meditation on Death

Meditators who have real, true, deep understanding and experience of impermanence and death are never shocked when they hear "renounce this life." Those who realize impermanence and death are only too happy to practice that which is the most powerful and beneficial way to stop delusions—no matter how difficult.

The Truth of Impermanence

We often feel afraid of death—when we are in an accident, when we are sick, when death comes to someone near us—but these feelings don't last. It is not enough to bring up a feeling of fear of death for just a couple of minutes or once a while; that is not the point. It is necessary to make the genuine wholesome fear of death last for more than a few minutes, more than an hour. Why? Because you can't complete the practice of Dharma in an hour. You have to make that wholesome fear last until you know you can be reborn according to your choice, or at least until you are fully confident of having achieved the very lowest purpose of this meditation, which is not suffering at the time of death. Without the wholesome fear of death, sometimes you might meditate for a couple of minutes and then let your mind go off on a picnic. But if you have deeply seen, understood, and realized impermanence, your mind will be so strong that this sort of thing will never happen; your mind will never be easily distracted. If you haven't experienced impermanence through meditation, if you don't have this realization, then any little problem will disturb your meditation.

Meditators who have real, true, deep understanding and experience of impermanence and death are never shocked when they hear "renounce this life." Such words only please their minds. Those who realize impermanence and death are only too happy to practice that which is the most powerful and beneficial way to stop delusions— no matter how difficult.

Since meditation is meant to stop your problems, you need to know how to do it, so practicing for just a day or two is not enough to learn; hearing someone explain something once and then just working on that is also not enough. You need to practice continually, again, and again, and again—constantly drawing your mind back to the truth of impermanence, the truth of death…your death.

The Nine-Point Meditation on Death

The Tibetan Buddhist tradition contains an extremely effective meditation on death called the nine-point meditation on death. It is presented with three root truths, three reasons for each truth, and three conclusions that follow from them:

Root: *Death is certain.*
No being has ever escaped death.
I am constantly becoming closer to death.
There is not much time to practice Dharma.
Conclusion: *I must practice Dharma.*

Root: *The time of death is uncertain.*
The lifespan of human beings is not fixed.
More conditions endanger life than support it.
This body is extremely fragile.
Conclusion: *I must practice Dharma* now.

Root: *Nothing can help at the time of death except my Dharma practice.*
Wealth can't help.
Friends and relatives can't help.
Your body can't help.
Conclusion: *I must practice Dharma* purely.

In the next few chapters, we'll look more deeply into each of the root truths, and how to work with this meditation.

When meditating on the above topics, see which parts are more effective for your mind, and focus on those. Focus on the parts that are more effective for you and then amplify them according to your own wisdom and experience in order to see things more clearly.

The Truth that Death Is Definite

Death is certain, definite, because no being has ever existed in the realms of samsara without continuously suffering death and rebirth. At this moment, if I really check up within myself, I can find neither evidence nor guarantee that my life will continue for any preordained period.

Reflecting on this, think from the depths of your being, "After some time, this whole world will become completely empty. I too will cease to exist on this earth." Feel the complete impermanence and voidness of all these things and conclude, "Therefore, death is definite."

Think, "There is no cooperative cause or condition that can stop death; there is no external condition that can stop death. As it has not been possible to prevent death from the time the world began until now, death is definite." Bring to mind your own life when thinking these thoughts.

"*My own* death will occur before I have had much time to spend practicing Dharma. Nothing external can prevent it, and when the time comes for me to die, even the best hospitals and all medicines, known and yet to be known, will not change this. No matter where I go, I can't escape my own death.

"Reflecting on my ancestors, from my parents, to my parents' parents, their parents, and on and on back through time, I see they all age and die. Even if my parents or grandparents or even great-grandparents are now alive, all the previous generations before them have gone; not one of them remains." Think of your ancestors who have died, and then reflect: "Therefore, it is certain that I will also die. Just as they have ceased to exist, so will I. Soon it will be my turn to die. Therefore, the fact of my death is certain."

The Truth that the Time
of Death Is Uncertain

Although the fact of death is definite, we can never know when it will come. The time of death is uncertain, indefinite. Consider these examples:

> People come to the East from the West but there is no certainty that they will return. Before it is time to return, they die. The time of death is uncertain in this way.

> Even though they might have returned to the West, they die before getting home.

> Many people go to sleep but die before they awaken.

> Many people start a meal but die before they finish.

> Many people go out by car but die before returning home.

> Many people are born but die before reaching adulthood.

> Many people go out to play sports but die before the game is over.

> Many people buy new clothes but die before they wear them.

> Many people start to read a book but die before they finish.

Many people plan a project but die before they can complete it.

Many people go to war but die before they they can come back.

Many people go to work but die before they collect their salary.

Many people breathe out but die before they can breathe in.

These are just a few examples of how the actual time of death is uncertain. Just as you see these things happening around you, it is necessary for you to see those examples in yourself, to reflect that what is happening to others can happen to you. Just as you see others dying before they have time to finish what they are doing, you have to see the same thing happening to you.

It is certain that you are going to die either during the day or night, in the morning or the afternoon or evening or night, without finishing something. You breathe out but die before you can breathe back in. According to your karma, you will surely die at some time or some other time, in some place or some other place.

You also have to think how our worldly needs can become the cause of death; how there are more conditions that endanger life than support it. Even such things as food and shelter can bring about the end of life. People die while eating meat or fish, when a bone becomes stuck in their throat. Others die when a house collapses on them. Some are killed by others in arguments over money or in drunken brawls. Others accidentally overdose on drugs. Even things that are supposed to support life can destroy it.

This body is extremely fragile, like a water bubble. Even a slight movement can cause injury. For this reason, too, know that the time of death is indefinite.

After all, can you really be sure of still being alive tomorrow? You subtly think that you will live for a long time, at least till next year, next week, tomorrow... until *later*. But is it definite that you will? Really check up on this; reflect deeply. Can you be sure of being alive *tonight*? Will you live long enough to go to bed?

Perhaps you think, "I have this intuitive, unspoken sense that I will continue to exist." In truth, even if you were going to die a minute from now, you would likely still have that feeling, that unspoken sense, wouldn't you? That instinctive feeling is a great hindrance to Dharma practice. And within Dharma practice it is a great hindrance to concentration.

Imagine a person walking through a tiger-infested forest. He is constantly aware of the danger of being attacked by a tiger, so he is always on the alert, always vigilant. He doesn't dare spend even a few minutes gazing at something without watching for tigers. It is the same with somebody who clearly realizes that the time of death is indefinite, uncertain, who always feels death might come today, in an hour or a minute. Because the person thinks, "I could die in any moment," he or she has a vast supply of great energy to make every action perfect and pure. Meditating with this thought, you won't have any hindrances to meditation; your mind won't be easily distracted. Your concentration will last much longer because this thought and the fear that comes with it does not allow you to fall under the control of hindrances.

The Truth of the Efficacy of the Dharma

Buddha Shakyamuni said: "It is uncertain whether tomorrow or the next life will come first. Therefore, it is more worthwhile and wise to be prepared for the future life than for tomorrow."

Since death is definite, it is certain that you will not exist forever; therefore, death is more certain than continued existence, even now. Thinking like this is very useful.

And because death is more definite than continued existence, even at this time, it is more profitable for you to do something that creates wholesome karma, something that benefits all beings and your future rebirths, rather than something for this body alone. Thinking like this is especially useful when you become angry, for example.

When you are having a mental problem with somebody—extreme greed, attachment to possessions or a person, anger, pride, or any other negative mind states—in order to stop creating negative karma and make your mind peaceful, to release confusion, try to think, "Shakyamuni Buddha taught that death is more likely than continued existence, so if I'm going to die right now, if my breath is going to stop the next time I breathe out, what's the use of being angry?" Why be angry, proud, or attached? There is no use whatsoever. All you are doing is creating suffering and the causes of suffering. Thinking like this is very useful.

If you reflect properly in this way, the uncomfortable feeling, the negative mind, will subside; you will be able to relax. You will clearly see there is no value in becoming angry; you will discover by yourself that it is meaningless. In this way, you won't cause problems for yourself or others; you will stop creating negative karma and confusion. This is real, practical meditation; this is using meditation in the actual critical time.

At the hour of death, no possessions, no wealth can keep death away; even the entire Pacific Ocean filled with numberless jewels cannot prevent death from occurring. No loved ones, relatives, or friends can hold death back, nor can any amount of personal strength.

At the time of death, we realize that we are separating from our possessions and loved ones, and tremendously strong attachment and fear arise.

At the hour of death, the king and the beggar are exactly equal; no people or possessions can affect or prevent death. So who is the richer at the time of death? If the beggar has created more merit, then although he looks materially poor he is really the rich person, rich in the Dharma. From the Dharma point of view, the mind that has prepared itself for the journey into rebirth has the real riches.

All our lives we have been attached to the physical body, providing it with all life's comforts, yet still it continues to cause us problems. The physical body creates much suffering and, although we have cared more for it than for any other being's body, it now becomes like our own enemy. Why is your body described as an enemy? Because as you feel that you are going to separate from it, you become extremely anxious; you don't want to leave it and this creates the causes of suffering. Instead of helping you solve your problem at that time, strong attachment to your body only causes you to remain longer in samsara, to always be trapped in the circle of the bondage of suffering, rebirth, and death. And the same trouble and worry you have with your body—attachment, fear of leaving it, not wanting to do so—you have with your possessions and relatives; you feel very upset at having to leave them.

Only the Dharma can help at the time of death; truly, only the Dharma can help before the time of death as well.

Ripples on a Lake

The great sage Padmasambhava said: "The vision of this life is like last night's dream. All meaningless actions are like ripples on a lake."

The dream you had last night was so short; from beginning to end, it was over so quickly. In a dream you might feel as if you have been on a long journey or spent many years doing something, but actually, a dream is just a few minutes in duration. Whatever good things happen in a dream are also over quickly. This is one reason why Padmasambhava likens life to a dream—they both finish so quickly. Life is over so soon, like a dream.

No matter what you enjoy in a dream, when you awaken, it is all gone. You might dream that you were successful in business, that you made billions of dollars and you feel so happy, but when you wake up, not a single dollar remains. Everything you do in a dream is of no use. In exactly the same way, no matter what you do in this life—how much money you make, how many possessions you accumulate, how successful your business, how happy you are—it is all like last night's dream. Not a single atom of it can be carried into your next life. Just as what you do in a dream is ultimately ineffective, so too are all the things you do for just this life alone. When you wake up, the dream is gone. When you die, all your comforts are gone.

Ripples on a lake come and go.

The Death of the Buddha

When Shakyamuni Buddha passed away, he took off his robes, lay down, and said to his disciples, "This is the tathagata's last holy body, so you must look at it." A *tathagata* is a being who has gone beyond all suffering and illusory mind; it is the way the Buddha is referring to himself. Lying down, he gave his last teaching: "All causative phenomena are impermanent. This is the last teaching of the tathagata." Then he passed away; he died.

This was his last teaching; this was his bequest to all of us, to all beings. This was the most important thing he had to leave for us—a teaching on impermanence. When he asked his disciples to look at the last holy body of the tathagata, many of them fainted and some arhats even passed away themselves; they couldn't bear his passing.

The very last thing he left, his very last teaching—like a will that ordinary people leave that talks of worldly things, the most precious things to the ordinary dying person—the most important and beneficial thing that Shakyamuni Buddha could bequeath, the most important thing for us to realize and understand, is the truth and reality of impermanence. Therefore, Buddha ended his life with a teaching on impermanence; his entire teaching career ended with this. This one word, impermanence, captures the full range of samsaric suffering.

Thus, you should practice Dharma because you are living in suffering, living in impermanence, under the control of death.

Remembering the Deaths of Those You've Known

When you are meditating on death, another useful technique is to remember, even to count up, all your relatives and friends who have died. Earlier, we meditated mainly on the generations of ancestors who had passed away, but here I am talking about those you actually met in this life.

Many of my own relatives and friends of this life have passed away—lay people, monks, lamas, and many other friends. I never knew my grandfather, even as a small child. I remember only my grandmother—gray hair, rosary, always sitting by the kitchen fire. She was often sick and later went blind. My uncle looked after her for many years, giving her food, taking her out to the bathroom, bringing her back in. He offered service to his mother for a long time, and in between taking care of her, he did prostrations. During that time, while he was taking care of his mother, she died.

Then there is my father. About the time I was due to come out of my mother's womb he had already gone to his next rebirth. When I was very small, all of us children would sleep together at night under our father's long-sleeved coat—his *chuba*, as it is called in Tibetan. It was made of animal hide with fur inside. We all slept under our dead father's coat, and sometimes we would say, "This belonged to Dad."

My mother had several other children, but many of them died

before I was born. Now there are just three of us left. Soon all these will also be gone and only their names will remain, with people saying, "Such-and-such a person did this," where nobody can see their physical body any longer. Later, even their names won't remain.

A Story of Realizing Impermanence

Then there is the first Western pen friend I had, when I was in India. Our schoolteacher was a Buddhist nun; I think she must have been one of the first Western nuns. Originally she was Christian, then later she traveled around Ceylon, where she took precepts from a Theravadan teacher, and then she went to India, where she lived and worked. Around this time, the Tibetan uprising of 1959 occurred and many Tibetans escaped to India. This nun was among those sent by the relief committee of the Indian government to look after the Tibetan refugees. Where she worked, the refugees were mainly monks from Lhasa.

One of the ways in which she helped the monks was by finding them pen friends in the West with whom they could correspond. The pen friend she found for me was a Jewish lady living in London. Sometimes she would send me photos of herself, some when she was young and some as she was at the time, which was very old. I was confused because I was quite young and didn't know which one was her. I didn't realize that they were pictures of the same person; I thought they were two different people. So little was my understanding of aging and impermanence at that age!

People recognized her as having a good personality and being wise. I think she also wrote books, although I didn't read any of them. She wrote me letters for seven years; each week, so many letters. My room was full of her letters. I replied only occasionally; maybe only three or four times altogether. She was more than eighty-seven, but at that time there wasn't much I could do to help her. She really wanted to understand Dharma, but I couldn't communicate much in English myself, and there weren't any other Tibetans at that place who could write well in English either.

Then her flood of letters stopped and I wondered what had happened. I think she thought that if she told me that she was going into the hospital for an operation, I would worry; that is why she didn't write. When she got out of the hospital she tried to write but her handwriting was no good; she didn't have the strength to form the letters properly. She couldn't even finish the letter she was writing and had some girl help her complete it. That was the last one I got, where she said she had just been released from the hospital.

After that, I had a dream that I was near my house and someone handed me a white letter. The next day, I received a letter exactly like that from her friend, who was the pen friend of another lama, explaining that she had died. Then the more than one thousand monks and high lamas who lived there prayed for her to find a better rebirth.

Around that time I'd sent her a gift, but I'm not sure she received it. She was cremated and her ashes were scattered outside in her garden. She gave the paintings I had sent her from India to a local Tibetan center before her death. This is just a little story of impermanence realized in my own life.

The Time to Practice Is Now

Just as death happens to other people, the same thing will happen to us.

Our first Western student, the nun Zina, was planning to come to Kathmandu and Dharamsala to receive teachings from our gurus; she made many plans to do all these precious things. However, just before it was time for her to come down from the mountains where she was in retreat, she suddenly got sick. Three or four days later, she was dead. While she was ill for those few days, she lay down in bed, but just before she died, she sat up, holding her rosary in her hand. Her daughter was there, looking her in the face and crying, "Please, mother, don't die."

Even though Zina was sick, she had a little time to prepare for death. She was fully expecting to do all the things she planned, but all of a sudden her life finished, before she had time to do them. Still, she was very lucky she could die as a nun. She died in a very simple, tiny room, having spent most of the previous year in retreat. Also, she had the constant wish to help other people, especially Westerners, but was always worried that she was incapable of doing so.

She wasn't even able to sign the last letter she sent us.

The fact of death is certain. The time of death is uncertain. At the moment of death, only your Dharma practice will help.

Please remember this.

The Five Powers

Bodhichitta, practicing the good heart, is the most important practice for someone committed to live a life of Dharma—but another practice described as the "five powers" is a close second. It might even be the most crucial. These powers should be practiced not only at the time of death or as death approaches rapidly, but throughout the entirety of one's life. In some ways, the five powers give a description of life lived for others, a Dharma life of constantly destroying the self-cherishing thought. The five powers are: the power of the "white seed"; the power of intention; the power of blaming the ego; the power of prayer; and the power of training. Let's look a little more deeply at *each of these*.

The first power, *the power of the white seed*, is the power that comes from relinquishing all of your attachments so that you can die without any sense of regret or worry for the future. This is fundamentally a practice of generosity, of giving everything away—all merit and all possessions—in the spirit of bodhichitta to Buddha, Dharma, and Sangha, and to all beings. By letting go of all these things, your mind becomes free to do various necessary meditations at the time of death.

This is a crucial practice of compassion. If the mind is trained in compassion, in bodhichitta, there is no question that people can bring much peace and happiness into their own life. They can also bring much peace and happiness to their family, neighbors, the area and country where they live, to the whole world and to numberless beings in other universes. There are countless benefits of the power of the white seed.

The second power is *the power of intention*. This refers to cultivating the thought, the aspiration, that from this very moment until the time that you ultimately attain enlightenment—from this point on—you vow to never let yourself come under the control of the self-cherishing thought, and furthermore, you vow to never become separate from bodhichitta.

When forming the intention that is at the heart of the second power, think to yourself:

> "I will never give self-grasping, delusions, and the nearing delusions any chance to arise. I will never allow my conduct of body, speech, and mind to be under the control of these obscuring, disturbing emotional thoughts. I will not allow myself to come under the control of self-cherishing, from now on until I die, and especially today. And I will never separate from bodhichitta, from now until I achieve enlightenment, from now until I die, and especially this year, this month—especially every moment of today."

The third power is *the power of blaming the ego*. This can also be thought of as the power of determination to subdue one's self-cherishing, to subdue each and every self-cherishing thought that arises. It is important to recognize that the ego, the self-cherishing thought, is the source of all suffering, all harm in the world. It is the most destructive thought imaginable. Each self-cherishing thought is like a burning coal or a blazing fire. The great teacher Shantideva says:

> As long as you don't drop the fire,
> The burning won't stop.

In the same way, as long as you don't let go of the I,
Suffering can't be abandoned.

And Nagarjuna, another peerless Indian master, says something similar:

When a fire spark jumps on one's head or clothing, immediately one shakes it off and throws it away, not allowing
it to remain there for a second. Like that, engage in the
practice of immediately abandoning the self-cherishing
thought the moment it arises.

So, do not to allow yourself to come under the control of the self-cherishing thought; kick it out immediately, cast it off, and renounce from the heart the great demon of self-cherishing.

The fourth power is *the power of prayer*. This does not refer to an easy or comfortable kind of prayer; it doesn't mean praying to be born in the Pure Land or some heavenly realm. It means praying to take upon yourself alone all the sufferings, all the myriad different defilements, obscurations, and all the negative karmas of all beings everywhere; and it means praying to generate bodhichitta.

To pray in this way you should think to yourself: "May I be able to remember bodhichitta my whole life, at the time of death, in the intermediate state, and at all times in the future."

The fifth power is *the power of training*. In an important way, this power encompasses all the other powers. It is the power of training that will enable you to bring all of your Dharma practice to bear at the very moment of death, and in the intermediate state and after. Ultimately, the power of training is also related to the transfer of con-sciousness at the time of death. Yet most essential for mastering the power of training is training in bodhichitta, becoming thoroughly habituated to using your mind in that way. Also important at the time of death is taking up the lion's pose, lying on the right side when one is passing away, just as the Buddha did as he passed into the sorrowless state. Even just doing this simple action can transform the moment of death positively. Doing this is a recollection of the Buddha, a practice which is virtuous by its very nature, and doing such virtuous practice helps free you from the control of self-cherishing.

SECTION 3

The Process of Dying

These visions, including the clear-light vision, also occur between sleeping and dreaming, and between dreaming and awakening, but they pass very quickly. The great meditators first practice here.

Dissolution of the Elements and Aggregates; Visions at the Time of Death

At the time of death, the elements that make up our physical bodies—earth, water, wind, and fire—are absorbed into each other, one after the other, dissolving into each other. Because of this, many changes appear to the dying person as feelings and visions. At the time of death, the mind separates from the body. The final moment of death comes when the most subtle mind splits from the body, and this also is accompanied by physical signs, about which I'll speak more below.

The person who has created much non-virtuous karma suffers disturbing hallucinations that are the result of his or her past negative actions. A person dying with an indifferent mind, neither virtuous nor non-virtuous, experiences neither pleasure nor suffering. A very frightening physical situation occurs because of these fearsome visions. A person who has created virtuous karma experiences a peaceful death.

For this reason, you should practice Dharma now, cultivate bodhichitta now, create wholesome karma now.

The process of a natural death—which is to say, a death that is not sudden or traumatic—proceeds like this:

First, the aggregate of form dissolves. At the same time, the great mirror wisdom—our ability to clearly see many objects at the same time, as a mirror reflects many objects together—also dissolves.

The earth element dissolves, and the physical body becomes very thin and loses power, the hands and legs become very loose, and we feel very uncontrolled, as if being buried under a great weight of earth.

Our eye sense-base dissolves, and it becomes impossible to control or move our eyes.

Finally, the "inner subtle form" dissolves. The color of the physical body fades and the body loses its strength completely. Internally, we see a trembling silver-blue mirage, like water in the heat.

Next, the aggregate of feeling dissolves. Our bodies no longer experience physical pleasure, pain, or indifference. At the same time, the wisdom of equality, of equanimity, which sees all feelings of happiness, suffering, and indifference as having the same nature, dissolves. We no longer remember those feelings perceived with the sense of mind as distinct from those perceived by the physical body.

The water element is absorbed, and all the liquids of the body— urine, blood, saliva, sperm, sweat, and so on—dry up. The ear sense-base dissolves and we can no longer hear. The inner sound is absorbed, and we no longer hear even the usual buzzing in the ears. Internally, we experience a vision of smoke, like the room is filled with incense.

Next, the aggregate of perception dissolves. We no longer recognize our relatives and friends or know their names. Along with that, the wisdom of discriminating awareness dissolves, and the fire element is absorbed.

The heat of the physical body disappears and the capacity to digest food ceases. The nose sense-base dissolves and inhaling becomes difficult and weaker, while exhaling becomes stronger and longer. The inner sense of smell is absorbed and our nose no longer detects smells. Internally, we experience a vision of sparks of fire, trembling like starlight.

Then the aggregate of compounded phenomena dissolves. Our

bodies can no longer move. At the same time, the all-accomplishing wisdom is absorbed. This is the wisdom of attainment that remembers outer work and success and their necessity. We lose the idea of the necessity and purpose of outer work.

The air element is absorbed and our breathing ceases. The taste sense-base also dissolves, and the tongue contracts and thickens and its root turns blue, and we no longer perceive soft nor rough sensations. The inner taste sense is absorbed, and we can no longer detect the six different tastes. Internally, we experience a vision of a dim red-blue light, like the last flickering of a candle.

Finally, the aggregate of consciousness dissolves.

This consists of the eighty gross superstitions and their foundation, motion. "Superstitions" here means the gross illusive mind, the dualistic, wrong-conception mind.

At the last moment before death, all of this dissolves.

Then, at the moment of death, we have the following visions.

First we see the white vision, which is like a very clear sky, like that in autumn, full of the brightness of the moon. Then we experience the red vision, which is like a copper-red reflection in the sky. Then we experience the dark vision, which is a vision of empty darkness, like a dark and empty space. Lastly, we experience the clear-light vision. This is a vision of complete emptiness, very clear, like the sky of an autumn dawn.

This is the vision of the final death. At this time, the time of actual death, the gross mind—that which holds gross objects—ceases, but only momentarily. Due to past karma, the seed of it is always there. It is possible that ordinary people stay in this stage for some time, but don't recognize it. Highly realized yogis are able to recognize all the visions of the death process.

As you can see, different visions come and go: mirage, smoke, sparks, flame. Now white vision, like an autumn moon rising or snow on the ground; then red; then dark, like the complete darkness of a dark room, like you are suddenly falling into darkness.

After the dark vision comes the clear-light vision of emptiness. But this is not *shunyata*; this is not that emptiness. If it were, it would be an effortless realization, achieved without meditation. It is not shunyata, but an emptiness like that of the sky at dawn, devoid or empty of the white, red, and dark visions.

If you have practiced Dharma vigorously, at this point there is a great opportunity.

Ordinary Deaths and the Deaths of Great Yogis

Many Tibetan lamas have passed away in meditation since coming to India. Ordinary Indian people never believed that such things as passing away while sitting in meditation were possible because they never saw it happen. Their usual concept was that the moment a person died, he or she should be taken out and cremated, burned on a pyre. In India, many sick Tibetan monks get taken to the hospital and, if they died there, it was difficult to convince the hospitals to leave the bodies of the monks alone for a while. They would want the body taken out immediately. The modern medical concept is that as soon as the breath stops, the person is dead. But this is not so.

During that time, there is no smell of decay. They smell the same as when they were alive. And in fact, they look magnificent, totally different from an ordinary person dying. Ordinary people—those who didn't practice Dharma during their life, who didn't purify their karma well, and who created many negative actions—appear very afraid when they die. Their eyes get wide and they cry because they have many fearful visions. They thrash their limbs about, move their hands as if they are trying to grab hold of something, and might become incontinent.

For great yogis, even after the breath stops, many remarkable visions take place.

What Great Yogis Experience
at the Time of Death

Generally, it is not permitted to openly give the details of what I will shortly mention, but I can tell you this: at this point in the death process, the yogis—those meditators who have spent their lifetimes in meditation and practiced various tantric methods, who have observed karma well and kept their precepts purely—use the methods they have been practicing all their lives. This is the moment they have been waiting for. They can remain in meditation in the clear light for many days or even weeks. The duration varies; it depends upon the meditator.

These visions, including the clear-light vision, also occur between sleeping and dreaming, and between dreaming and awakening, but they pass very quickly. All great meditators first practice here, in their dreams. Once they can control their dreams, they know for sure that they will be able to employ these profound methods during their actual death. And similarly, you yourself can discern from your own inability to do this during sleep how impossible it will be for you to be conscious enough to practice these methods during death, to be conscious enough to recognize the visions as they evolve during the death process.

All these visions, including the clear light, are ordinary occurrences that all beings experience—unless their death is sudden, as in an accident, murder, and so forth. Even ordinary people experience the gradual absorption of the eighty gross superstitions after the breathing stops, before the white, red, and dark visions occur. The dark vision occurs when the very subtle mind is enclosed in the seed at the heart.

This seed, like a tiny bean, is composed of two hemispheres. The moment of death occurs when this seed opens and the very subtle mind leaves the body. The sign that this has happened is that a trickle of red blood comes out of the person's nose and a white fluid exudes from the sex organ. It usually takes up to three days for all this to happen (although with certain diseases, these fluids don't come out). When the great meditators have completed their meditation, the red and white fluids come out.

The Intermediate-State Body

Usually however, for those who have not practiced Dharma, because of our attachment to the self, as the cognition weakens during the death process, the wrong concept arises that "I am becoming non-existent." This, then, causes fear of losing the I. These thoughts create attachment to and craving for the body, which in turn leads to birth in the intermediate state, the state between the death of this life and the birth of the next life.

As a person enters the intermediate state, the visions that occurred during the death process re-occur but in the reverse order: dark, then red, then white. Then the eighty superstitions arise.

The intermediate-state body is not a body of form, thus it is indestructible, like a vajra, like a diamond. It has no physical resistance and so nothing can resist it; it can pass through all things in the bardo and all things can pass through it. It also has certain karmically derived psychic powers, such as being able to instantly arrive wherever it thinks of being. But, for those who do not attain realization, who have not thoroughly purified their karma and obscurations, it also undergoes much suffering like, for example, feeling as if it is buried under ground and being pressed down by huge mountains.

The intermediate-state body has illusory visions, but not realizing that these are projected by its own mind, it experiences fear. It feels as if it is being blown about uncontrollably from place to place by a strong red wind or a fierce storm, or caught in a noisy fire, or drowning in an ocean with huge, wrathful waves. It might see karmically created *yamas*—monsters with terrifying bodies and fearful animal heads—chasing it, shouting, trying to beat and destroy it. It has many frightening experiences like these.

There is no time to relax in the intermediate state; there is so much fear and suffering.

For this reason, the time to practice Dharma is now.

SECTION 4

Meditations and Dedications

The most important practice is bodhichitta. You should remember bodhichitta every day and be ready to die on any day, because indeed death can happen at any time. This is my advice to you regarding the fear of death.

Die with Bodhichitta

Dying with bodhichitta is the best way to die. Always keep this in mind. Keep repeating, "I am going to die for the benefit of all beings. This death, and all the Dharma practice, and all the service, that I am doing and have done is for the benefit of all beings."

All during the day, every day, you should live with a bodhichitta motivation. Live your life to serve others. Think, "I'm here to free all beings from samsara, from suffering, and lead them to enlightenment, bringing them happiness in this life and in all future lives and liberation from samsara."

Throughout the day, it is very good to think in this way: "The purpose of my life is not only my own happiness, not only solving my own problems. The goal of my life is to free others from suffering and to cause all the happiness—temporal and ultimate—to benefit others. I'm just one living being among countless others. My importance is small. How much I suffer or how much happiness I achieve is small. There are numberless other beings who want happiness, who don't want suffering and who need my help. Every one of them is the source of all my past, present, and future happiness. Each of them is the most precious one in my life. How incredibly fortunate I am that I can let go of my self—from which all problems and all the undesirable things come—and instead cherish others and experience their death and all their problems for them. I can let them have all the temporal and ultimate happiness."

The key thing is always to make a resolution early in the morning not to be controlled by self-cherishing thoughts, resolving that, "From now on, until death, especially today, I will never be separated from bodhichitta." The rest of the day, by putting all your effort into it, try to do all your other activities with that thought. When you create meritorious karma each day, dedicate it to actualizing bodhichitta, both for yourself and for all beings. Dedicate it in order to be able to generate bodhichitta in this life and all future lives. Study the teachings on bodhichitta so you can see that it has great meaning in your life. Knowing the extensive benefits, you can enjoy your life practicing bodhichitta.

Thinking in this way will enable you to die in the correct way, the most beneficial way. These thoughts make even death—your last experience of life—beneficial for others, which is the most crucial thing.

So when you find out you are going to die, put all your effort into generating bodhichitta, giving beings all your happiness, merit, and possessions. Meditate that they receive all this, and that it causes them to actualize the path and achieve enlightenment. Do this while generating great loving-kindness, wishing them to have happiness, and wishing that you cause them to have it. Then generate compassion and take on their suffering, their sickness, and especially their death. This is related to the practice of *tonglen*.

Tonglen—The Practice of Taking and Giving

One of the best practices to prepare for death is *tonglen*, the practice of "taking and giving." In this meditation, we generate great compassion and take the suffering and causes of suffering of numberless other living beings upon ourselves. We use their suffering to destroy our self-cherishing thought, the source of all our problems. By generating great loving-kindness, we then give other beings everything we have: our possessions, our merit, our happiness—even our body and mind. We can do this practice whenever we have a problem, whether it is cancer or some other disease, the ending of a relationship, failure in business, or difficulty in our spiritual practice.

To practice tonglen, meditate that you take into yourself all the suffering and death of all other beings in the form of black smoke. Absorb this smoke through the nose and let it destroy the egocentric self-cherishing thought at your heart. The ego becomes nonexistent. If you can do this meditation, it's extremely good. Give your suffering, your illness, your cancer, or the very causes of your body's own death to your own self-cherishing, to your attachment, aversion, and ignorance, to your delusions.

If you are dying of cancer, for instance, consider that there are so many beings with cancer and other illnesses, so many more with the potential for cancer. Think to yourself, "I am going to die anyway, so I shall use my illness as a cause to benefit all beings, to generate bodhichitta. I will receive cancer and all beings' sufferings upon myself. So many times I have made this prayer to take all suffering to be experienced by myself alone, and now that prayer has come wondrously true." You can see the very cause of your death, cancer for instance, as the answer to your prayers of bodhichitta. Each time you have the thought, "I have cancer," think, "I am experiencing it for all beings." When your mind is depressed or weak, visualize that the cancer is destroying your ego, your worst enemy, the demon of self-ishness. At other times, when you are feeling more strength, experience the cancer for others. In this way, see your illness as the path to enlightenment, something important to have, even to cherish gratefully. More than that, your illness becomes a *necessity*. In this way, you purify and cease the defilements; you use your illness to purify the cause of your illness. Thus, the cancer or other condition that frightens the mind becomes medicine more powerful than any mantra.

Truly, this approach, this practice of tonglen, applies to every difficult circumstance of our lives—suffering, pain, illness, death; loss, change, fear—all of it. As long as we are in samsara, there is no way to be truly healthy in the sense of being truly free from suffering. It is as if we are living in a fire; we cannot expect not to be burned and to be comfortable. But even so we can practice tonglen in the face of every difficulty that we experience, from birth to death, and make our lives and all our difficulties of great benefit to ourselves and others.

Every time you think of experiencing suffering for others, you purify so much negative karma. Medical science does not do this, cannot help you do this. Medicine itself cannot cure the true cause of suffering; the more important thing is meditation.

To prepare for death, practice tonglen. Take the suffering of all beings into your heart, as you breathe in, and give them to your ego in order to destroy it. Give all these sufferings also to the emotional "I" that appears to really exist from its own side but is actually nonexistent. Try to die with this motivation. If you die with this bodhichitta thought, your death becomes a cause of your enlightenment and a cause for the enlightenment of all beings. Live your life with this precious thought, which is all-fulfilling for you and all-fulfilling for all beings.

In addition to using tonglen to generate bodhichitta, you can use it to destroy the self-cherishing thought.

Again: Imagine breathing in a thick black smoke. Imagine that this smoke is all the suffering of the world, all the harm that comes to all beings, all the pain and sickness everywhere. Also breathe in all the undesirable environments experienced by humans, animals, hungry ghosts, and the many suffering beings in the hell realms. Imagine breathing this in through your nostrils and let it be completely absorbed into the self-cherishing thought at your heart, completely destroying that self-cherishing thought with each breath.

Remember: It is your self-cherishing thought that interferes all the time with your immediate and ultimate happiness and with your ability to free all beings from all their sufferings and obscurations and to lead them to immediate and ultimate happiness.

As you breathe in this smoke and absorb it into your self-cherishing thought, the self-cherishing thought starts to become nonexistent. As the self-cherishing thought becomes nonexistent, so does the "real" I, the I existing from its own side, which the self-cherishing thought regards as so precious and important. Just as the self-cherishing thought becomes nonexistent, so does the object it cherishes.

All that is left there is what is merely imputed. This merely imputed I then breathes out happiness, and freedom, and light—and offers charity to other beings. The merely imputed I breathes out and offers everything—all your own happiness and merit, the causes of happiness; your own body; your possessions—to the hell beings, hungry ghosts, animals, humans, and the beings enjoying the heavens. Your body becomes a wish-granting jewel and you offer charity to all beings. All their environments become pure realms.

Clearly envision that those who need money receive wealth—each person owns the whole sky filled with money. Those who need a guru find a perfectly qualified teacher who can reveal the whole path to enlightenment to them. Those who need medicine receive it. Those who need a doctor, or a husband, or a wife, or a friend, find one. Each being receives whatever is needed for happiness.

Through this practice, all beings receive whatever they need, and all these enjoyments become the cause only to purify their minds and to generate in their minds the path to ultimate happiness, so that they all become fully enlightened beings. Imagine they all become Chenrezig—the Buddha of Compassion.

You can conclude tonglen by meditating for a little while on the emptiness of the I, maintaining awareness that the I is empty of existing from its own side.

The time just prior to death is crucial. Truly if we can manage to use the power of tonglen to transform our mind into bodhichitta and destroy the self-cherishing thought in those critical moments, truly that is better than winning a million-dollar lottery. Thus, rather than rejecting death as something to fear, we can use it to develop our mind in the path to enlightenment. If we cannot practice tonglen at the time of our death, we miss an incredible opportunity to benefit ourselves and all other beings.

Giving Your Body Away

This is a short meditation on thought transformation, in which we dedicate the four elements of our bodies to the happiness of all beings, putting into practice the action of renouncing self and cherishing others.

His Holiness the Dalai Lama often quotes the following verse from Shantideva's *A Guide to the Bodhisattva's Way of Life*:

> Just like space
> And the great elements such as earth
> [and water, fire, and air],
> May I always support the lives
> Of all the boundless creatures.

With this verse we are requesting to become the basis, the support, the very life-foundation of all the inconceivably vast number of beings—and not just briefly, for a moment or two or a few days, but forever. When we give away our bodies in this fashion, it is up to those other beings to decide how to use the elements of our bodies—the earth, water, fire, air, and space—for their happiness. It's not up to the elements to decide; it's not up to us.

To do this practice, imagine the following: First imagine that the four elements that form your own body absorb into the four external elements of earth, water, fire, and air. Imagine that your flesh and bones absorb into the external earth element. Imagine that your body becomes the stable earth and is used by all beings in whatever way they wish for their survival and happiness, not only in this world but in all worlds.

Imagine that your body is used by all beings as fields and crops; beautiful parks, roads, and vehicles; to obtain gold, diamonds, and other precious jewels; to build houses and cities; to make tunnels and bridges. Visualize this as elaborately as possible.

Your two eyes then become the sun and moon and work for all beings, illuminating them, guiding them. Your flesh becomes food for all beings. Visualize that your flesh absorbs into all the food in the world, all the food in all the supermarkets. You become pizzas, mozzarella cheese, macaroni, hamburgers, momos—and all beings everywhere are eating you. Again, it is important to think of not just one being in this world, but of all beings in every world. Give your skin to all beings—let your skin become the clothes that beings are wearing, or the hair or fur or feathers that keep them warm.

Visualize the blood, water, and other liquids in your body absorbing into the external water element, which is also used by all beings for their survival and happiness. Think of the many different ways in which the water of the world, which is none other than your own body's fluids, is used by beings for their happiness. Again, visualize as extensively as possible the many different uses of water— it floods rice paddies, it flows through irrigation canals, it nourishes flowers, it appears as nectar, it quenches thirst everywhere. Beings are drinking you as orange juice, Coca-Cola, alcohol, mother's milk, Gatorade.

Next, imagine that the internal heat of your body absorbs into the external fire element, which is used by all beings for their happiness. Think of how heat and the ability to burn benefit all beings—heat keeps them warm, it gives them light, it creates energy; heat is used for cooking and survival, for safety and exploration. As always, imagine this as extensively as possible, in as much detail as possible.

Your breath absorbs into the external air, the wind element, which is used by all beings for their survival through breathing and moving. Wind is light in nature and enables movement, grants freedom. Breath is life itself. Let yourself be breathed in by all beings, bringing life-sustaining oxygen to every cell in the body of every being.

Now imagine that all the sufferings and negative karmas of all beings everywhere ripen upon you—and thereby know that all beings are freed from all their suffering and its causes, all their negative karmas and obscurations.

Let all the harmful karma of all beings everywhere come to fruition, and let yourself receive all the results. Absorb all this suffering and all its causes into your own self-cherishing thought, destroying that thought and the object it cherishes, the "real" I. Now even the real I, which appears to exist from its own side, becomes empty.

All that is left is the merely imputed I, and this one now dedicates all your happiness and merit to all beings. All the beings in each realm receive and experience your past, present, and future happiness and merit. In the same way, also dedicate all the merit of the buddhas and bodhisattvas throughout space and time. Know that this merit is also received and experienced by all beings.

In this way, your body, composed of the four elements, becomes nectar—and into this nectar of your body flows the transcendental wisdom from the hearts of all the buddhas and bodhisattvas. The essence of all the worlds is also absorbed into the nectar. And this nectar nourishes and supports all beings, immediately fulfilling all their wishes, giving them ultimate happiness, ultimate joy.

And now, since you have offered your body to all beings of the six realms, it no longer exists. All that is left now is your mind, which doesn't have natural existence, which doesn't exist from its own side.

Focus on its actual nature, its emptiness. Bring to awareness the fact that the mind doesn't have the slightest existence from its own side, that it's completely empty.

Now recite OM AH HUM seven times.

Then dedicate the merit.

Dedicating Merit

The best way to dedicate merit is to dedicate it to achieve enlightenment for all beings. When you do this, that merit becomes inexhaustible, unceasing. A very important point when you dedicate merit is to also dedicate it in the purest way, by "sealing it with emptiness." By specifically concentrating on the meaning of "mere imputation," the emptiness of all things from their own side, you make your dedication in a way that is pure and unstained by the concept of true existence. Doing this, sealing your dedication with emptiness, renders it indestructible—it will never be destroyed by any future greed, anger, or wrong views. Sealing the dedication with emptiness gives great protection, like storing your money or possessions in an uncrackable, disaster-proof safe.

To dedicate merit, think to yourself: "Due to the merits of the three times—past, present, and future—accumulated by me and by all other beings, may bodhichitta, the good heart, the source of all happiness and success, be generated in my own mind and in the minds of all other beings. May those who have already generated bodhichitta increase it."

And then, to seal the dedication with emptiness, think to yourself: "Due to all the merits of the three times, which are merely imputed, accumulated by me and by all other beings, which are merely imputed, may the I, which is merely imputed, achieve enlightenment, which is merely imputed, and lead all beings, who are merely imputed, to enlightenment, which is merely imputed."

Conclusion

His Holiness the Dalai Lama says that it is difficult at the time of death to really meditate as you did in life. If during your life you couldn't meditate well, then you won't be able to meditate at death; you won't be able to hold concentration.

The essence, therefore, is to have accumulated merit and done purification in everyday life in your relationship with all beings; with a sincere heart, loving-kindness, and compassion to have served others; and to have done the hard work to benefit them.

Practicing the good heart, bodhichitta, during your life purifies so much negative karma, even very heavy karma, and it stops you from creating more. It is negative karma that makes the mind experience fear of death, and it is bodhichitta especially that stops the immeasurable suffering and the suffering rebirths that arise later from these negative actions.

More Meditations

Meditation on Impermanence

Preparation

Sit in a comfortable position, with your back straight, and let your body relax. Spend some time letting your mind settle down in the present moment. Let go of thoughts of the past or the future. Make the decision to keep your mind focused on the meditation-topic for the duration of the meditation session.

Motivation

When your mind is calm and settled in the present, generate a positive motivation for doing the meditation. For example, you can think: "May this meditation help bring about greater peace and happiness for all beings," or: "May this meditation be a cause for me to become enlightened so that I can help all beings become free of suffering and become enlightened as well."

The Meditation

The Buddha said that all produced things are impermanent, that is, they change moment by moment. "Produced things" doesn't refer only to things produced in a factory like cars or shoes, but includes all things that arise from causes and conditions, such as plants, trees, animals and insects, mountains and oceans, as well as our bodies and minds. All these things do not remain the same from one moment to the next, but are constantly changing. This isn't just a philosophical theory, but a fact of life; the actual way things exist. Through not being aware of or accepting this reality of things, we become attached to people and things—wishing them to remain the same and last forever—and then become deeply disappointed when they do not. Making ourselves familiar with their impermanence enables us to be more realistic and frees us from a great deal of unnecessary suffering, and this meditation will help us to do that.

Begin the meditation by observing your breathing, and slowly become aware of the impermanence of your breathing. Each breath is different from the one that came before it, and is different from the one that comes after it. You are breathing in different air with each breath, and your body is changing with each breath: there are different sensations around the nose and inside the nostrils; your lungs expand and contract, your abdomen rises and falls. So in each moment, with each breath, there is change, flux, and flow.

Then think about other changes that are taking place in your body in each moment. Think of how your body is made of many different parts—arms, legs, head, skin, blood, bones, nerves, and muscles—and how these parts themselves are made of yet smaller parts, such as cells. Be aware of the movement that is going on each moment: the beating of your heart, the flow of your blood and the energy of your nerve-impulses. On a more subtle level, neurons are firing, cells are being born, disintegrating, and dying.

On an even subtler level, all the parts of your body are made of molecules, atoms, and sub-atomic particles, and these are in constant motion. Try to really get a feeling for the changes that are taking place each moment in your body.

Then turn your attention to your mind. It too is composed of many parts—thoughts, perceptions, feelings, memories, images—following one after the other, ceaselessly. Spend a few minutes simply observing the ever-changing flow of experiences in your mind, like someone looking out of a window onto a busy street, watching the cars and pedestrians passing by. Don't cling to anything that you see in your mind, don't judge or make comments—just observe, and try to get a sense of the impermanent, ever-changing nature of your mind.

After reflecting on the impermanence of your inner world—your own body and mind—extend your awareness to the outer world. Think about your immediate surroundings: the cushion, mat, or bed you are sitting on; the floor, walls, windows, and ceiling of the room you are sitting in; the furniture and other objects in the room. Consider that each of these things, although appearing solid and static, is actually a mass of tiny particles whizzing around in space. Stay with that awareness of the impermanent, constantly changing nature of these things.

Then let your awareness travel further out, beyond the walls of your room. Think of other people: their bodies and minds are also constantly changing, not staying the same for even one moment. The same is true of all living beings, such as animals, birds, and insects.

Think of all the inanimate objects in the world and in the universe: houses, buildings, roads, cars, trees, mountains, oceans and rivers, the earth itself, the sun, moon, and stars. All of these things, being composed of atoms and other minute particles, are constantly changing, every moment, every nanosecond. Nothing stays the same without changing.

While you are meditating, if at any point you experience a clear, strong feeling of the ever-changing nature of things, stop the thinking or analyzing process, and hold your attention firmly on this feeling. Concentrate on it for as long as possible, without thinking of anything else or letting your mind be distracted. When the feeling fades or your attention starts to wander, again return to analyzing the impermanent nature of things.

Conclusion

Conclude the meditation with the thought that it is unrealistic and self-defeating to cling to things as though they were permanent. Whatever is beautiful and pleasing will change and eventually disappear, so we can't expect it to give us lasting happiness. Also, whatever is unpleasant or disturbing won't last forever—it might even change for the better!—so there's no need to be so upset about it or to reject it.

Finally, dedicate the positive energy from doing the meditation that all beings will find perfect happiness and freedom from all suffering.

Meditation on the Inevitability of Death

Preparation

Sit in a comfortable position, with your back straight, and let your body relax. Spend some time letting your mind settle down in the present moment; let go of thoughts of the past or the future. Make the decision to keep your mind focused on the meditation-topic for the duration of the meditation session.

Motivation

When your mind is calm and settled in the present, generate a positive motivation for doing the meditation. For example, you can think: "May this meditation help bring about greater peace and happiness for all beings," or: "May this meditation be a cause for me to become enlightened so that I can help all beings become free of suffering and become enlightened as well."

The Meditation

As you contemplate the following points, use your own ideas and experiences, as well as stories you have heard or read, to illustrate each point. Try to get a feeling of each point. If at any time during the meditation you experience a strong, intuitive feeling of the point you are examining, stop thinking and hold the feeling with concentration as long as you can. When it fades or your mind gets distracted, return to the contemplation.

We plan many activities and projects for the coming days, months, and years. Although death is the only event that is certain to occur, we don't usually think about it or plan for it. Even if the thought of death does arise in our mind, we usually push it away quickly—we don't want to think about death. But it's important to think about and be prepared for it. Contemplate the following three points to get a sense of how death is definitely going to happen to you.

1. EVERYONE HAS TO DIE

To generate an experience of death's inevitability, bring to mind people from the past: famous rulers and writers, musicians, philosophers, saints, scientists, criminals, and ordinary people. These people were once alive—they worked, thought, and wrote; they loved and fought, enjoyed life and suffered. And finally they died.

Can you think of an example of someone who was born on this earth but who did not die?

No matter how wise, wealthy, powerful, or popular a person may be, his or her life must come to an end. The same is true for all other living creatures. For all the advances in science and medicine, no one has found a cure for death, and no one ever will.

Now bring to mind people you know who have already died.... And think of the people you know who are still alive. Contemplate that each of these people will one day die. And so will you....

There are several billion people on the planet right now, but one hundred years from now, all of these people—with the exception of a few who are now very young—will be gone. You yourself will be dead. Try to experience this fact with your entire being.

2. YOUR LIFESPAN IS DECREASING CONTINUOUSLY

Time never stands still—it is continuously passing. Seconds become minutes, minutes become hours, hours become days, days become years, and as time is passing in this way, you are traveling closer and closer toward death. Imagine an hourglass, with the sand running into the bottom. The time you have to live is like these grains of sand, continuously running out.... Hold your awareness for a while on the experience of this uninterrupted flow of time carrying you to the end of your life.

Another way to get a sense of your life moving continuously toward death is to imagine being on a train which is always traveling at a steady speed—it never slows down or stops, and there is no way that you can get off. This train is continuously bringing you closer and closer to its destination: the end of your life. Try to really get a sense of this, and check what thoughts and feelings arise in your mind.

3. THE AMOUNT OF TIME YOU HAVE FOR SPIRITUAL PRACTICE IS VERY SMALL

Since you are getting closer and closer to death all the time, what are you doing to prepare for it? The best way to prepare for death is doing spiritual practice. This is because the only thing that continues after death is the mind, and spiritual practice is the only thing that truly benefits the mind, preparing it for death and the journey to the next life. But how much time do you actually devote to spiritual practice—working on decreasing the negative aspects of the mind (such as anger and attachment) and developing the positive aspects of the mind (such as kindness and wisdom), and behaving in ways that are beneficial to others?

Calculate how you spend your time: In an average day, how

many hours do you sleep? How many hours do you work? How many hours do you spend preparing food, eating, and socializing? How much time do you spend feeling depressed, frustrated, bored, angry, resentful, jealous, lazy, or critical? And how much time do you spend consciously trying to improve your state of mind, or doing beneficial things such as helping others, or spiritual study or meditation? Do these calculations honestly.

Assess your life in this practical way to see clearly just how much of your time is spent doing things that truly benefit yourself and others, and that will be helpful for your mind at the time of death and in the next life.

By meditating on these three points, you should be able to develop the determination to use your life wisely and mindfully.

Conclusion

Conclude the meditation with the optimistic thought that you have every possibility to make your life meaningful, beneficial, and positive, and in this way you will be able to die with peace of mind. Remember the motivation you had at the beginning of the meditation and dedicate the merit of doing the meditation to that same purpose—for the benefit of all beings.

Meditation on the Uncertainty
of the Time of Death

Preparation

Sit in a comfortable position, with your back straight, and let your body relax. Spend some time letting your mind settle down in the present moment; let go of thoughts of the past or the future. Make the decision to keep your mind focused on the meditation-topic for the duration of the meditation session.

Motivation

When your mind is calm and settled in the present, generate a positive motivation for doing the meditation. For example, you can think: "May this meditation help bring about greater peace and happiness for all beings," or: "May this meditation be a cause for me to become enlightened so that I can help all beings become free of suffering and become enlightened as well."

The Meditation

As you contemplate the following points, use your own ideas and experiences, as well as stories you have heard or read, to illustrate each point. Try to get a feeling of each point. If at any time during the meditation you experience a strong, intuitive feeling of the point you are examining, stop thinking and hold the feeling with concentration as long as you can. When it fades or your mind gets distracted, return to the contemplation.

By contemplating the inevitability of death (the first root), you come to accept that you are definitely going to die. But you might think that death is not going to happen for a long time. Why do you think this? Is there any way you can know for sure when death will happen? Contemplate the following three points to get a sense of how the time of death is completely uncertain and unknown.

1. HUMAN LIFE-EXPECTANCY IS UNCERTAIN

If human beings died at a specific age, say eighty-eight, we would have plenty of time to prepare for death. But there is no such certainty, and death catches most of us by surprise.

Life can end at any point: at birth, in childhood, in adolescence, at the age of twenty-two or thirty-five or fifty or ninety-four. Think of examples of people you know or have heard about who died at different ages.... Think of people who died before they reached the age you are now at....

Being young and healthy is no guarantee that a person will live a long time—children sometimes die before their parents. Healthy people can die before those who are suffering from a terminal illness such as cancer.... We can hope to live until we are seventy or eighty, but we cannot be certain of doing so. We cannot be certain that we will not die later today.

It is very difficult to feel convinced that death could happen at any moment. We tend to feel that since we have survived so far, our continuation is secure. But thousands of people die every day, and few of them expected to. Generate a strong feeling of the complete uncertainty of your own time of death; how there is simply no guarantee that you have long to live.

2. THERE ARE MANY CAUSES OF DEATH

There are many different ways that death happens to people. Sometimes it happens due to external causes. These include natural disasters such as earthquakes, floods, and volcanic eruptions, or accidents such as car or plane crashes. People can also be killed by other people—murderers or terrorists—or by dangerous animals or poisonous insects. Bring to mind examples you have heard or read about.

Death can also happen due to internal causes. There are hundreds of different diseases that can rob us of our health and lead to death. There are also cases of people who are not ill, but something goes wrong in their bodies and they suddenly die, in their sleep or while working. And then there is old age; no one is safe from that. Again, think of specific examples of people who died in these ways.

Even things which normally support life can become the cause of death. Food, for example, is something we need in order to stay alive, but it can sometimes lead to death, as when people overeat, or eat contaminated food. Medicine normally supports life, but people sometimes die because they took the wrong medicine, or the wrong dose. Houses and apartments enable us to live comfortably, but they sometimes catch fire or collapse, killing the people inside.

People die in their sleep, in the womb, coming home from work, going to school, on the playing field, cooking dinner. Death can occur at any time, in any situation. Bring to mind cases of people you know or have heard about who have died, and think of how they died. Think that any of these things could happen to you as well.

3. THE HUMAN BODY IS VERY FRAGILE

Our human body is very vulnerable; it can be injured or struck down by illness so easily.

Within minutes it can change from being strong and active to being helplessly weak and full of pain.

Right now you might feel healthy, energetic, and secure, but something as small as a virus or as insignificant as a thorn could drain your strength and lead to your death. Think about this.

Recall the times you have hurt or injured your body, and how easily it could happen again and even cause your death. Your body won't last forever. In the course of your life you might manage to avoid illness and accidents, but the years will eventually overtake you—your body will degenerate, lose its beauty and vitality, and finally die.

By meditating on these three points, you can develop the determination to begin your practice of the spiritual path right now, as the future is so uncertain.

Conclusion

Conclude the meditation with the optimistic thought that you have every possibility to make your life meaningful, beneficial, and positive, and in this way you will be able to die with peace of mind. Remember the motivation you had at the beginning of the meditation and dedicate the merit of doing the meditation to that same purpose—for the benefit of all beings.

Meditation on What
Helps at the Time of Death

Preparation

Sit in a comfortable position, with your back straight, and let your body relax. Spend some time letting your mind settle down in the present moment; let go of thoughts of the past or the future. Make the decision to keep your mind focused on the meditation-topic for the duration of the meditation session.

Motivation

When your mind is calm and settled in the present, generate a positive motivation for doing the meditation. For example, you can think: "May this meditation help bring about greater peace and happiness for all beings," or: "May this meditation be a cause for me to become enlightened so that I can help all beings become free of suffering and become enlightened as well."

The Meditation

As you contemplate the following points, use your own ideas and experiences, as well as stories you have heard or read, to illustrate each point. Try to get a feeling of each point. If at any time during the meditation you experience a strong, intuitive feeling of the point you are examining, stop thinking and hold the feeling with concentration as long as you can. When it fades or your mind gets distracted, return to the contemplation.

No matter how much we have acquired or developed throughout our life—in terms of family and friends, wealth, power, travel experiences, and so on—none of it goes with us at death. Only our mind continues, carrying imprints of all that we have thought, felt, said, and done. It is vital that when we die, we will have as many positive imprints—the cause of good experiences—and as few negative imprints—the cause of suffering—on our mind as possible. Also, we should aim to die at peace with ourselves, feeling good about how we lived our life, and not leaving behind any unresolved conflicts with people.

The only things that will truly benefit us at the time of death are positive states of mind such as faith, non-attachment, calm acceptance of the changes that are taking place, loving-kindness, compassion, patience, and wisdom. But in order to be able to have such states of mind at the time of death, we need to make ourselves familiar with them during the course of our life—and this is the essence of Dharma, or spiritual practice. Realizing this will give us the incentive and energy to start practicing Dharma now, and to practice as much as we can while we still have time.

You can experience a strong feeling of this reality by imagining yourself at the time of death, and contemplating the following three points:

I. YOUR LOVED ONES CANNOT HELP

When you face difficult or frightening situations, your thoughts usually turn to loved ones: your family and friends. So it is natural that you would wish them to be with you when you die. However, it's not certain that they will be there—you might die far from home.

But even if they were present with you at the time of death, would they be able to help you? Although they love you very much and do not want you to die, they cannot prevent this from happening. Also, it is possible that they wouldn't know what to say or do that will give you peace-of-mind; instead, their sadness and worry about the coming separation would probably stir up the same emotions in your mind.

When we die, we go alone—no one, not even our closest, dearest loved one, can accompany us. And being unable to accept this and let go of our attachment to our loved ones will cause our mind to be in turmoil and make it very difficult to have a peaceful death.

Recognize the attachment you have to your family and friends. Try to realize that having strong attachment to people can be a hindrance to having a peaceful state of mind at the time of death, so it is better to work on decreasing this attachment and learning to let go.

2. YOUR POSSESSIONS AND ENJOYMENTS CANNOT HELP

Your mind will probably also think of your possessions and property, which occupy a great deal of your time while you are alive, and are a source of much pleasure and satisfaction. But can any of these things bring you comfort and peace at the time of death? Your wealth may be able to provide you with a private room in the hospital and the best medical care, but that is all it can do for you. It cannot stop death from happening, and when you die, you cannot take any of it with you—not even one cent. Not only will your possessions be unable to help you at the time of death, but your mind may be caught up in worries about them—who will get what, and whether or not they will take proper care of "your" things. So that will make it difficult to have a peaceful, detached state of mind as you are dying. Contemplate these points, and see if you can understand the importance of learning to be less dependent on and attached to material things.

3. YOUR OWN BODY CANNOT HELP

Your body has been your constant companion since birth. You know it more intimately than anything or anyone else. You have cared for it and protected it, worried about it, kept it comfortable and healthy, fed it and cleaned it, and experienced pleasure and pain with it. It has been your most treasured possession. But now you are dying and that means you will be separated from it. It will become weak and eventually quite useless: your mind will separate from it and it will be taken to the cemetery or crematorium. What good can it possibly do you now?

Contemplate the strong sense of dependence and attachment you have to your own body, and how it cannot benefit you in any way at death. Fear of pain and regret about leaving it will only compound your suffering.

By meditating on the final three points, try to realize how important it is to work on reducing your attachment to the things of this life, such as family and friends, possessions, and your body. Realize how important it is to take care of your mind, as that is the only thing that will continue to the next life. "Taking care of the mind" means working on decreasing the negative states of mind such as anger and attachment, and cultivating positive qualities such as faith, loving-kindness, compassion, patience, and wisdom.

Furthermore, as the imprints of your actions in this life will also go with your mind to the next one, and will determine the kind of rebirth and experiences you will have, resolve that you will try your best to refrain from negative actions, and create positive actions as much as possible during your life.

It is possible that you will feel fear or sadness when doing this meditation. In one sense, that is good—it shows that you have taken the ideas seriously and have contemplated them well. Also, it is important to get in touch with how you do feel about death so that you can work on being prepared for it when it happens. However, the purpose of the meditation is not to make you frightened. Just being afraid of death is not helpful. What is helpful is to be afraid of dying with a negative state of mind and a lot of imprints on your mind from negative actions you have done in your life. You need to get a strong sense of how terrible it would be to die like that, so that you live your life wisely, doing as many positive, beneficial things as possible.

Also, fear arises because of clinging to the idea of a permanent self—there is no such thing, so this is a delusion that just makes us suffer. If we keep death in mind in an easy, open way, this clinging will gradually loosen, allowing us to be mindful and make every action positive and beneficial, for ourselves and others. And awareness of death gives us enormous energy to not waste our life, but to live it as effectively as possible.

Conclusion

Conclude the meditation with the optimistic thought that you have every possibility to make your life meaningful, beneficial, and positive, and in this way you will be able to die with peace of mind. Remember the motivation you had at the beginning of the meditation and dedicate the merit of doing the meditation to that same purpose—for the benefit of all beings.

OM AH HUM Purification Meditation

(A meditation to purify our body, speech, and mind)

from "Life, Death, and After Death" by Lama Thubten Yeshe

Preparation

Sit comfortably and relax your body. Relax your mind by letting go
of or putting aside any other thoughts—of the past or future, people,
activities, etc. Decide to keep your attention focused on the meditation for the duration of the session.

Motivation

When your mind is calm and settled in the present, generate a positive motivation for doing the meditation. For example, you can
think: "May this meditation help bring about greater peace and happiness for all beings," or: "May this meditation be a cause for me to
become enlightened so that I can help all beings become free from
suffering and become enlightened as well."

The Meditation

Visualize a white OM in the center of your brain. Recognize that the
OM is the pure energy of the divine body of the buddhas and bodhisattvas, or whoever you think is pure.

Recite "OM" slowly for several minutes. While reciting it, visualize that white light radiates from the OM in your head and fills your body. All your conceptions and the impure energy of your body are cleansed and purified. (You can think of specific negative actions you have done—such as killing or harming another being, stealing, or unwise sexual behavior—and feel that the imprints of these actions are completely purified.) Your entire body, from your feet up to the top of your head, is completely filled with radiant, blissful white energy. Really feel this….

When you stop chanting "OM," stay for a while in silence, and just be aware—not thinking anything is good or bad, not reacting, not making mental conversation. Just place all your attention on the light consciousness at the center of your brain. Be there. Be intensely aware and let go—without sluggishness, without distraction.

Now visualize a red AH at your throat chakra. It looks similar to the sun when it is setting. Recognize that the AH is the pure speech energy of the buddhas and bodhisattvas.

As you recite "AH" slowly for several minutes, visualize that red light radiates from the AH at your throat, and your entire body is embraced by this blissful radiating light energy. It purifies your speech. Purification means that the uncontrolled mind and speech work interdependently with each other. Negativities of speech mean harming and giving pain to others through lying, slander, harsh speech, and gossip. You can imagine that the imprints of your negative actions of speech are completely purified by the blissful red light. Having a clean, clear mind and controlled speech is the way to purify impure and uncontrolled speech.

After reciting "AH" for several minutes, let your mind just be in the state of intense awareness on your own consciousness. Stay there without any expectation or interpretation. Comprehend your experience of the non-dual, non-self-existent I, nothingness, zero, empty space as truth, reality. This experience is much more real than the waking fantasy of your sensory world.

If an uncontrolled, distracted thought comes, remember that not only you, but all other sentient beings are in this situation, so cultivate much loving-kindness for others. Then, when loving-kindness arises, direct intense awareness of loving-kindness toward your own consciousness.

So there are two things: place intense awareness on your own consciousness, and when distractions arise, generate loving-kindness for all beings and then direct intense awareness of loving-kindness to your consciousness. Alternate these two.

Next, visualize your loving-kindness energy manifesting at your heart chakra in the aspect of a full moon.

Visualize at your heart, on a moon disc, a blue radiating HUM. Recognize that this is the non-duality wisdom of the buddhas' and bodhisattvas' energy. Your heart is pure, cool, and calm, opened by the radiating light of the moon and HUM. Infinite blue light radiates from the HUM, and fills your entire body. Your entire body feels blissful. All narrow thoughts disappear. All indecisive minds disappear. All obsessed minds disappear. Being embraced by the infinite blue light leaves no room for fanatical, dualistic concepts. Visualize this while reciting "HUM" slowly for a few minutes.

After this, feel infinite blue light, like your consciousness, embracing the entire universal reality. Your intense awareness is embracing the entire universal reality. Feel and be, without any expectation or superstition.

We need two experiences: wisdom and method. Wisdom experience is intense awareness of your own conscious reality. This is the way of wisdom. Method is when you again become out of control, distracted. That distracted experience is a big resource to again generate loving-kindness. When there is no distraction, stay in the wisdom. So, two things: when there is no problem, place your attention on the wisdom aspect; when you are distracted, switch to method, which is loving-kindness. Meditate like this for as long as you wish.

Conclusion

Conclude your meditation by dedicating the merit, or positive energy, of doing the meditation to all living beings: may it be the cause for all beings to be free of their suffering and its causes—uncontrolled, disturbing states of mind—and may they all attain perfect peace and happiness.

Meditation on the Four Opponent Powers

(To purify past negative or unwholesome karma)

Preparation

Sit comfortably and relax. Spend some time focusing on the breath to calm your mind and center it in the present.

Motivation

Then generate a positive motivation for doing the practice, for example, "I am doing this meditation not just for myself, but for others— to learn to be less harmful, and more helpful, to them."

The Meditation

Take as much time as you need to contemplate each of the four powers thoroughly, to generate the right state of mind for each point.

I. THE POWER OF REGRET

Think back over the day, from the time you woke up this morning, or over the last day or two, and try to remember anything you did that was negative. Start with actions of the body, such as killing or causing physical suffering to any being... taking something that did

not belong to you, or not paying money you owed, like a bus fare...
or engaging in inappropriate sexual behavior.... Then check if you
did anything negative with your speech, such as lying, exaggerating,
or being deceitful, saying words that caused bad feelings between
people, saying things that were hurtful or upsetting to someone, or
spending time gossiping or talking about insignificant things. Then
see if you can remember negative thoughts you may have indulged
in, such as wishing harm to someone or feeling happy at his or her
misfortune... critical, judgmental thoughts toward anyone, including yourself... feeling dissatisfied with what you have and wishing
for more or better, or for what someone else has—in short, any
states of mind that involved hatred, anger, greed, jealousy, arrogance,
selfishness, and so forth. Also bring to mind any negative actions
you recall doing in past days, months, and years, going as far back in
your life as you can. Generate sincere regret, from the depths of your
heart, for all these actions, by understanding that they are the cause
of suffering—in some cases, to others, and in all cases, to yourself.
These actions planted imprints on your mind that will ripen as
problems and misfortune in the future. They also impede your
progress on the spiritual path, and prolong your existence in an
imperfect, unsatisfactory situation. Realize that no one wants to suffer, and these are the very things that bring suffering. Acknowledge
your mistakes and feel a sincere wish to rectify them.

2. THE POWER OF RELIANCE

Bring to mind a holy being or higher power who is endowed with
unconditional love, compassion, and wisdom, and toward whom you
feel respect and confidence. For example, if you are a Buddhist, this
would be the Three Jewels of Refuge; if you are Christian, this would
be God or Jesus; and so forth. Alternatively, you can bring to mind
the ethical principles that you believe in and try to follow in your life.

Then acknowledge your mistakes and ask for help and guidance to be able to change yourself and give up unskillful behavior from now on. Renew your commitment to follow your objects of refuge and/or your ethical principles to the best of your ability.

For the unskillful and harmful actions you did to others, generate love and compassion. Contemplate the fact that, just like you, others wish to not suffer and wish to experience only happiness and peace. Feel how desirable it would be if you could stop harming them and instead be kind and helpful to them. Generate the altruistic wish to purify your negative actions and your delusions such as anger, greed, and selfishness, so that from now on you can only benefit others, not harm them.

3. THE POWER OF REMEDY

Now you need to do something positive to counteract the negative energy you created.

A standard practice in Tibetan Buddhism is to visualize an enlightened being, such as the Buddha, Chenrezig, or Vajrasattva, above your head. You then take refuge and recite the appropriate mantra* while imagining light flowing down from the figure, filling your entire body and mind and purifying all your negative karma and delusions.

Alternatively, you can do a meditation to generate a positive state of mind, such as love, compassion, or patience. Another recommended practice is to read and reflect on the meaning of spiritual texts.

You can also do more engaged activities such as volunteer work to help the poor and needy, or making donations to charitable causes.

* The mantras are: *tadyatha om muni muni maha muniye svaha* for Shakyamuni Buddha, *om mani padme hum* for Chenrezig, and *om vajrasattva hum* for Vajrasattva.

Saving lives—for example, rescuing animals or insects who are in danger of dying or being killed, or caring for the ill—is particularly effective to counteract the karma of killing or harming others. If possible, you can also apologize and make amends to the people you have harmed.

4. THE POWER OF RESOLVE

If you feel confident that you can completely give up some negative actions, such as killing and stealing, make the promise to do that. But for those negative actions you cannot completely give up, either promise to give them up for a realistic period of time, or promise that you will do your very best to be mindful and avoid doing them.

Resolve to change your old emotional habits such as anger, jealousy, depression, criticalness, and attachment. Feel confident in your ability to change, but at the same time understand that it takes time to change, so don't have unrealistic expectations.

Dedication

At the end of the meditation session dedicate all the positive energy you have created by doing this purification practice to all living beings, that they may become free from all their suffering and its causes: negative karma and delusions.

Tonglen Using One's Own Problem

Preparation

Sit comfortably and relax your body. Relax your mind by letting go of or putting aside any other thoughts—of the past or future, people, activities, etc. Decide to keep your attention focused on the meditation for the duration of the session.

Motivation

When your mind is calm and settled in the present, generate a positive motivation for doing the meditation. For example, you can think: "May this meditation help bring about greater peace and happiness for all beings," or: "May this meditation be a cause for me to become enlightened so that I can help all beings become free from suffering and become enlightened as well."

The Meditation

Bring to mind a problem you are having. It could be a physical problem such as sickness, pain, or discomfort; or an emotional problem such as a feeling of depression, loneliness, or anxiety. It could be a problem you are having at work, or in a relationship.... Focus on your problem: allow it to arise in your mind, feel how painful it is, and how your mind wants to push it away.... Then think: "I am not the only person experiencing a problem like this. There are many others...." Think of other people who may be experiencing the same problem, or something similar to it. There may be some people who experience this kind of problem to an even greater degree than yourself (for example, if you have lost a loved one, think of people who have lost many loved ones, in a war or natural disaster).

Then generate compassion, thinking: "How wonderful it would be if all those people could be free from their suffering." Make the decision that you will accept or take on your own experience of this problem, in order that all those other people can be free from theirs. You can do this with the breath: visualize breathing in others' suffering in the form of dark smoke. It comes into your heart, where the self-cherishing mind is located, in the form of a solid, dark spot or rock. The dark smoke of suffering absorbs into the rock of self-cherishing and destroys it... Then breathe out happiness, positive qualities, and merit, in the form of bright light, giving to yourself and all those other people whatever they need in terms of resources and qualities to be able to deal with the problem and to progress along the path to enlightenment. Imagine that they actually receive all these things, and feel a sense of joy and peace.

Conclusion

When you wish to conclude the meditation, remember the motivation you started with, and dedicate the positive energy of doing the meditation to the happiness and enlightenment of all beings.

Tonglen for Another Person's Problem

Preparation

Sit comfortably and relax your body. Relax your mind by letting go of or putting aside any other thoughts—of the past or future, people, activities, etc. Decide to keep your attention focused on the meditation for the duration of the session.

Motivation

When your mind is calm and settled in the present, generate a positive motivation for doing the meditation. For example, you can think: "May this meditation help bring about greater peace and happiness for all beings," or: "May this meditation be a cause for me to become enlightened so that I can help all beings become free from suffering and become enlightened as well."

The Meditation

Imagine in front of you someone you know and love who is suffering. Put yourself in their situation, and try to really feel the suffering they are experiencing and how they wish to be free of it. Feel how wonderful it would be if they could be free from all their suffering and problems. Then generate the courage to take their suffering upon yourself.

Visualize that your delusions such as self-centeredness, anger, attachment, and jealousy are in the form of a solid, dark rock in your heart. Then visualize your loved one's suffering in the form of thick, dark smoke floating out of his or her body. As you inhale, imagine taking this dark smoke of suffering into yourself. It comes to your heart, absorbs into the rock of self-centeredness and delusions, and destroys it. Both the rock and the suffering, your own and that of the other person, become utterly non-existent. Feel a sense of joy that this person is now free from his or her suffering and problems....

When you exhale, breathe out your happiness, positive qualities, and merit in the form of bright light. Imagine that it transforms into whatever will bring joy and peace of mind to this person, such as the things they need and wish for to be happy and healthy, satisfying relationships, inner qualities such as love, compassion, courage, and equanimity, and so on. Imagine that their needs and wishes are fulfilled, their mind is filled with peace, happiness, and all the knowledge and qualities of the spiritual path. Let your mind rest for some time in a feeling of joyfulness that you have been able to help your loved one in this way.

As you become more familiar with this meditation, you can practice it gradually with more of your friends and relatives, then strangers, and eventually even with those you dislike.

Conclusion

When you wish to conclude the meditation, remember the motivation you started with, and dedicate the positive energy of doing the meditation to the happiness and enlightenment of all beings.

Medicine Buddha Meditation

Note: This practice can be done for yourself, or for another person who is ill, dying, or in need of help, in which case you would visualize the Medicine Buddha above that person's head. Lama Zopa Rinpoche says that the main practice to do before, during, and after death is that of the Medicine Buddha.

Preparation

Sit comfortably with your back straight. Take a few minutes to settle your mind into the present moment by focusing on your breathing, and letting go of all other thoughts....

Motivation

Generate a positive motivation for doing the practice. Lama Zopa Rinpoche says that healing practice is most effective when done with an altruistic motivation. You can generate such a motivation by thinking, "I am going to do this practice in order to help all beings become free from sufferings such as disease, as well as from the causes of sufferings: delusions and karma."

The Meditation

Visualize the Medicine Buddha a few inches above the top of your head. He is sitting on a moon disc which rests in the center of an opened lotus, with his legs crossed in the vajra, or full-lotus position, and faces the same way as you. His body is made of bright royal-blue light, the color of lapis lazuli. Every aspect of the visualization is made of light and radiates light. His right hand rests on his right knee in the gesture of granting sublime realizations and holds the stem of an arura (myrobalan) plant between his thumb and first finger. His left hand, in his lap, is in the gesture of concentration and holds a lapis lazuli bowl filled with nectar. He wears the three saffron robes of a monk, and has all the signs and marks of a fully-enlightened buddha. His face is peaceful and smiling, looking at all living beings in the universe with compassion and loving-kindness.

Spend some time contemplating the visualization of the Medicine Buddha. Understand that he is the embodiment of all enlightened beings and their sublime qualities. Feel the peace and compassion emanating from him.

If you wish, you can recite the following prayers to generate devotion to the Medicine Buddha and the wish to become a Buddha yourself to benefit all beings:

PRAYER OF REFUGE AND BODHICHITTA

> I go for refuge until I am enlightened
> To the Buddha, the Dharma, and the Supreme Assembly.
> By my practice of giving and other perfections,
> May I become a Buddha to benefit all sentient beings.
> (repeat 3 times)

THE FOUR IMMEASURABLE THOUGHTS

> May all sentient beings have happiness and the causes of
> happiness;
> May all sentient beings be free from suffering and the
> causes of suffering;
> May all sentient beings be inseparable from the happiness
> that is free from suffering;
> May all sentient beings abide in equanimity,
> free from attachment and anger that hold some close and
> others distant.

PRAYER TO THE MEDICINE BUDDHA

> To the bhagavan, tathagata, arhat, fully enlightened Buddha
> Medicine Guru, King of Lapis Light, I prostrate, go for
> refuge, and make offerings. May your vow to benefit sen-
> tient beings now ripen for myself and others. (repeat 7
> times)

Then visualize infinite rays of radiant white light flowing down from the heart and body of the Medicine Buddha. This light fills your body and purifies all disease, afflictions due to spirits or black magic, as well as the causes of these problems: your negative karma, delusions, and mental obscurations. All these negativities leave your body in the form of thick black liquid, like black oil. Your body becomes as clean and clear as crystal. You can also imagine that all other beings are being purified in the same way. Do this visualization while reciting the mantra of the Medicine Buddha:

> tadyatha / om bhaishajye bhaishajye maha bhaishajye
> bhaishajye / raja samudgate svaha

[common pronunciation: tayata om bhekandzye bhekandzye maha bhekandzye [bhekandzye] radza samudgate soha.]

Then recite the mantra again, as many times as you wish, and visualize that the light flowing from the Medicine Buddha fills your body again, bringing all the realizations of the path to enlightenment, and all the qualities of the buddhas and bodhisattvas. You can imagine that the same happens to all other beings. Feel that you and all other beings have actually received all these excellent qualities: that you have received the blessings and inspiration of the Medicine Buddha. Finally, visualize that the Medicine Buddha melts into light, which absorbs into your heart. Your mind becomes one with the enlightened mind of all buddhas. Let your mind rest for a while in a state that is completely clear, peaceful, and free from its usual busy thoughts and conceptions. Feel that this is your true nature.

Conclusion

To conclude, dedicate the merit, or positive energy, of the meditation that it will bring true physical and mental health and happiness to all sentient beings, and will be the cause for their eventual attainment of enlightenment.

Medicine Buddha

How to Begin
Meditating Right Now

adapted from How to Meditate *by Kathleen McDonald*

Advice for Beginners

In order to experience the benefits of meditation it is necessary to practice regularly; as with any activity, it is not possible to succeed unless we dedicate our energy wholeheartedly to it. Try to meditate every day, or at least several times a week. If you let weeks or months pass without meditating you will get out of shape and find it all the more difficult when you try again. Inevitably there will be times when the last thing you want to do is meditate, but meditate anyway, even for only a few minutes; often these sessions are the most productive.

If possible, it is best to reserve a room or corner especially for your meditation sessions.

Set up your seat, either a cushion on the floor, on a bed or sofa, or a straight-backed chair, with a table or low bench in front of you for this and other books that you need for your meditations.

If you are so inclined you can set up an altar nearby for statues or pictures that inspire you, and for offerings to the buddhas such as candles, incense, flowers, and fruit.

Ideally, the place should be clean and quiet, where you won't be disturbed. However, with discipline it is possible to meditate in a crowded, noisy environment; people in prison, for example, often cannot find a quiet place and still become successful meditators. Even if your surroundings are busy and noisy, make your meditation place as pleasing and comfortable as possible, so that you are happy to be there and can't wait to return!

It is good to start with the meditation on the breath. This is ideal for calming the mind and starting to develop some insight into your thoughts and feelings—and both calm and insight are essential ingredients for successful meditations of any kind.

In the beginning it is best to meditate for short periods—ten to thirty minutes—and end your session while mind and body are still comfortable and fresh. If you push yourself to meditate for too long and rise from your seat with an aching body and a frustrated mind, you won't have much interest in sitting down to meditate again. Meditation should be a satisfying and productive experience, not a burden. Decide beforehand on a period of time for the session and stick to it, even if the meditation is going well. As your skill develops you can increase the length of your sessions accordingly.

Since we all want to enjoy happiness and peace of mind and avoid problems, it is natural to want good experiences during meditation. But such expectations are not necessarily realistic and are likely to hinder your progress. The mind is complex and ever-changing. One day you might have a calm, joyful meditation and the next a meditation beset by distractions and turmoil. This is quite normal and should not cause worry or frustration. Be ready for anything and do not be disturbed by whatever happens. The most troublesome painful experiences can be the most valuable in terms of the growth of wisdom.

Feel satisfied that you are making the effort to meditate and transform your mind—that itself is meditation. As long as you are trying, it is mistaken to think that you can't meditate. Results take time. Don't be discouraged if you have not achieved good concentration within a few weeks; it is better to think in terms of years. Habits built up over a lifetime are not eliminated instantly but by gradual cultivation of new habits. So be easy on yourself. Recognize your capabilities and limitations and evaluate your progress accordingly.

Meditation is an internal, not external, activity. Your practice will transform your mind on a subtle level, making you more sensitive and clear, and giving you fresh insight into ordinary day-to-day experiences. Superficial changes are not natural and are unlikely to impress anyone, but the deep, natural changes created by meditation are real and beneficial, both for yourself and others.

As you begin, check up on your thoughts. Why do you want to meditate? What do you hope to achieve? As with any activity, the clearer and more firmly we set our goal, the stronger is our motivation and the more likely we are to succeed.

A short-term goal of meditation is simply to calm down and relax. More far-reaching is the aim eventually to penetrate through to a complete understanding of the nature of reality as an antidote to unhappiness and dissatisfaction. However, the most altruistic and thus the highest aim of meditation is to achieve enlightenment in order to help others gain it, too. It is the most far-reaching objective—the Mahayana motivation—and inevitably the other goals will be reached on the way. If you are comfortable with this idea, you can start your meditation by thinking: "I am going to do this meditation in order to attain enlightenment so that I can help all beings attain that state as well."

However, it may be difficult for you to think that your reason for meditating is to attain enlightenment—this goal may seem too vast or far-distant for you to realistically consider—but you may still have an altruistic wish to be more beneficial to others. In that case you could think something like this: "I wish to practice meditation in order to decrease the negative energy in my mind—anger, self-centeredness, attachment, pride, and so forth—and to increase my positive qualities such as love, compassion, patience, and wisdom. In this way, I will have more beneficial, positive energy to bring into my interactions with others, and to send out into the world."

Whichever your motivation, think it through clearly before proceeding with your meditation.

Now, turn to the object of meditation and keep it firmly in mind throughout the period. If you do a stabilizing meditation—for example, focusing on the breath—aim to hold your mind unwaveringly on the object of concentration.

If you do an analytical meditation, investigate the topic with full attention until an intuitive feeling of it arises, then place your mind single-pointedly—in other words, do stabilizing meditation—on that insight so that it becomes literally one with your experience. When the feeling or your concentration starts to fade, return to the analytical process.

End the analytical meditation with a firm conclusion about the topic, based on your insight and experiences during the session.

Whichever method you use, the important point is to be relaxed and free of all unrealistic expectations about the way you think the session should go. Follow the instructions—and your own wisdom—as well as you can, don't panic, and have confidence!

Posture

Mind and body are interdependent. Because the state of one affects the state of the other, a correct sitting posture is emphasized for meditation. The seven-point posture, used by experienced meditators for centuries, is recommended as the best:

LEGS. The ideal position for meditation is the *vajra*, or full-lotus, position, where you sit cross-legged with each foot placed, sole upward, on the thigh of the opposite leg. This position is difficult for many people, but practicing yoga or stretching exercises may loosen your legs enough to be able to sit this way for a short time, and continued practice will enable you to maintain it for increasingly longer periods. The vajra posture gives the best support to the body, but is not essential, so don't worry if you are unable to do it.

An alternative position is the half-lotus where the left foot is on the floor under the right leg and the right foot on top of the left thigh. You can also sit in a simple cross-legged posture with both feet on the floor.

Having a mat or carpet beneath you and a cushion or two under your buttocks will enable you to sit comfortably for longer periods, with a straight back, and avoid numbness in your legs and feet.

If you are unable to sit in any of these cross-legged positions, you can meditate in a chair or on a low, slanted bench. The important thing is to be comfortable.

ARMS. Hold your hands loosely on your lap, about two inches below the navel, right hand on top of the left, palms upward, with the fingers aligned. The two hands should be slightly cupped so that the tips of the thumbs meet to form a triangle. Shoulders and arms should be relaxed. Your arms should not be pressed against your body but held a few inches away to allow circulation of air: this helps to prevent sleepiness.

BACK. Your back is most important. It should be straight, held relaxed and lightly upright, as if the vertebrae were a pile of coins. It might be difficult in the beginning, but in time it will become natural and you will notice the benefits: your energy will flow more freely, you won't feel sluggish, and you will be able to sit comfortably in meditation for increasingly longer periods.

EYES. New meditators often find it easier to concentrate with their eyes fully closed. This is quite acceptable. However, it is recommended that you leave your eyes slightly open to admit a little light, and direct your gaze downward. Closing your eyes may be an invitation to sluggishness, sleep, or dream-like images, all of which hinder meditation.

JAW. Your jaw should be relaxed and teeth slightly apart, not clenched. Your mouth should also be relaxed, with the lips together lightly.

TONGUE. The tip of your tongue should touch the palate just behind the upper teeth. This reduces the flow of saliva and thus the need to swallow, both of which could be distracting as your concentration increases and you sit in meditation for longer periods.

HEAD. Your neck should be bent forward a little so that your gaze is directed naturally toward the floor in front of you. If your head is held too high you may have problems with mental wandering and agitation, and if dropped too low you could experience mental heaviness or sleepiness.

This seven-point posture is most conducive to clear, unobstructed contemplation. You might find it difficult in the beginning, but it is a good idea to check every point at the start of your session and try to maintain the correct posture for a few minutes. With familiarity it will feel more natural and you will begin to notice its benefits.

The practice of hatha yoga or other physical disciplines can be a great help in loosening tight muscles and joints, thus enabling you to sit more comfortably. However, if you are unable to adapt to sitting cross-legged you can make a compromise between perfect posture and a relaxed state. In other words, keep your body and mind happy, comfortable, and free of tension.

Meditation on the Breath

One useful kind of meditation, stabilizing meditation, is for the purpose of developing concentration. Concentration is a natural quality of our mind—we use it when we study, work, watch TV, or read a book. But our ability to concentrate is limited—our mind is easily distracted—and the things we concentrate on are not necessarily beneficial for ourselves and others. Concentration in itself is not positive—it depends on how we use it. A bank robber, for example, needs very good concentration to carry out his crime. As the goal of spiritual practice is freeing our mind from negative thoughts and emotions, and attaining perfect clarity, peace, and joy, we need to learn to concentrate our mind on positive, beneficial objects.

Stabilizing meditation involves focusing the mind on an object and bringing it back whenever it wanders away. Among the many objects recommended by the Buddha to use for developing concentration, the breath is one of the best. We are breathing all the time anyway, so we don't have to conjure up some object to focus our mind on. Also, as our breathing is happening right here, right now, focusing on it helps our mind stay in the present, the here-and-now, rather than getting lost in memories of the past or fantasies about the future. Following the breath with our attention has a naturally calming effect on our mind, thus quieting our normally busy thoughts. The fourteenth century Tibetan meditation master, Je Tsongkhapa, in his book *The Great Treatise on the Graduated Path to Enlightenment*, said that if you have a lot of discursiveness, you should definitely meditate on the breath.

There are several qualities of the mind that are essential in developing good concentration. One of these is mindfulness, or recollection, which enables us to remember a familiar object (like our breath) without forgetting it or wandering to other objects. Mindfulness also enables us to keep in mind what we're supposed to be doing while we are sitting there, and not to get completely spaced out!

Another essential quality is discriminating alertness, which, like a sentry, watches out for distractions. Alertness knows what's happening moment by moment—whether our mind is paying attention to the object of meditation, or has wandered off to something else. It is also able to recognize negative thoughts and emotions such as anger and desire, which disturb our mind and can lead to problems for ourselves and others. Developing the ability to recognize these when they arise in our mind and do something about them before they escalate helps us to avoid a lot of suffering.

Mindfulness and alertness are thus essential for successful meditation; and in our day-to-day lives they keep us centered, alert, and conscientious, helping us to know what is happening in our mind as it happens and thus to deal skillfully with problems as they arise.

You can use the meditation on the breath either for your main practice or as a preliminary to other meditations. It is an invaluable technique: regular practice helps you gradually become more aware of your inner world, and gain more control over your mind. You will feel more relaxed and more able to enjoy life, having greater sensitivity to yourself and the people and things around you. And using your increased mindfulness in other meditations, you will be able to maintain your concentration for longer periods.

Meditation on the breath, and stabilizing meditation in general, is therefore important for both beginners and advanced meditators:

for those who want a simple technique for relaxing and calming the mind and for serious meditators who devote their lives to spiritual development.

Begin by sitting in whatever position is most comfortable for you. Relax all your muscles and the other parts of your body, while keeping your back straight. If there is any tension in any part of your body, let it dissolve and disappear. Let your breathing be natural so that your breath flows in and out in a natural rhythm.

Motivation

Have a positive motivation for doing the meditation, for example, "I am going to meditate in order to generate in my mind more positive energy, and decrease the negative energy, for the benefit of myself and everyone else."

Decide how long you will meditate for (if you're a beginner, ten to thirty minutes is good; you can gradually increase the length of time as your concentration improves), and determine that for the duration of the session you will keep your attention on the breath in order to fulfill this purpose.

The Meditation

Now focus your mind on your breathing. You can do this either by focusing on the openings of your nostrils, where you can feel subtle sensations as the breath enters and leaves your body, or by focusing on the in-and-out movement of the abdomen with each breath.

Choose one of those two places, and keep your mind, your attention, on the sensations you can feel at that place during each inhalation and exhalation of your breath. Bring your mind back to this place every time it wanders away.

If you wish, you can count your breaths. You may find this helpful to keep your mind concentrated. You count each full inhalation and exhalation of the breath as one.

You can say to yourself, "Breathing in, breathing out, one. Breathing in, breathing out, two…" and so on. Count up to five or ten breaths, then start again at one. If your mind wanders in the middle of the counting, go back and start again at one. Continue counting in rounds of five or ten breaths, and bringing your attention back to the breath every time it wanders away. If your mind becomes more stable and is able to stay focused on the breath without needing to count, then you can dispense with the counting.

Don't try to control your breath; just breathe normally and gently. Inevitably, thoughts will appear, and your attention will be distracted by them, but as soon as you realize this has happened, bring your mind back to the breath.

Learn to have a neutral attitude toward your thoughts, being neither attracted nor repulsed. In other words, do not react with dislike, worry, excitement, or clinging to any thought, image, or feeling that arises. Merely notice its existence and return your attention to the breath. Even if you have to do this fifty times a minute, don't feel frustrated! Be patient and persistent; eventually your thoughts will subside.

It may be helpful to think that your mind is like the sky, and thoughts are like clouds. Clouds come and go in the sky—they do not stay long, nor do they alter the natural stillness and spaciousness of the sky. In the same way, thoughts come and go in the clear space of your mind; they are transient, momentary. If you can simply notice them and let them go, bringing your attention again and again to the breath, the thoughts will disappear on their own.

Be content to stay in the present. Accept whatever frame of mind you are in and whatever arises in your mind, without judging it as good or bad. Be free of expectation, clinging, and frustration. Have no wish to be somewhere else, to be doing something else, or even to feel some other way. Be content, just as you are.

When your skill has developed and your ability to avoid distractions has increased, you can take your alertness a step further. Make mental notes of the nature of the thoughts that arise, such as "thinking," "memory," "fantasy," "feeling angry," "attachment," "hearing a sound," "feeling bored," or "pain." As soon as you have noted the thought or feeling, let it go, recalling its impermanent nature.

Another technique is to use your distractions to help you gain insight into the nature of the mind. When a thought arises, instead of focusing on the thought itself, focus on the thinker. This means that one part of the mind, discriminating alertness, takes a look at another part, a distraction. The disturbing object will disappear, but hold your attention on the thinker for as long as you can. Again, when another thought comes, focus on the thinker and follow the same procedure. Return to watching the breath once the distractions have passed.

These methods for handling distractions can be applied to any meditation. It is no use ignoring or suppressing disturbing thoughts or negative energy, because they will recur persistently.

Conclusion

When it's time to end the session, feel good about what you have done. Don't judge your meditation with thoughts such as, "that was a lousy meditation; my mind was all over the place." Remember that just making the effort to meditate is in itself very meaningful and beneficial. Rejoice in the positive energy you have generated, and dedicate it to the benefit of all beings—may their minds may become free from problems and unhappiness, and be filled instead with peace and joy.

Appreciating Our Human Life

The function of analytical meditation is to help us recognize and cut through the mistaken attitudes and ideas that cause unhappiness and dissatisfaction. Our experiences in life depend upon how we think and feel about things, and because most of the time we do not perceive things the way they really are, we encounter one frustrating situation after another.

As long as we blame our parents, society, or other external factors, we will never find any satisfying solutions to our problems. Their main cause lies within our own mind, so we need to take responsibility for changing our way of thinking where it is mistaken, that is, where it brings unhappiness to ourselves and others.

This can be done through meditation, by gradually becoming aware of how we think and feel, distinguishing correct from incorrect attitudes, and finally counteracting harmful attitudes by the appropriate means.

The starting point for many problems is the way we feel about ourselves and our life. Human existence is very precious, but normally we fail to appreciate it. We have so much potential, so much latent wisdom and loving-kindness, so much to offer the world, but we may ignore or be unaware of this and let ourselves become clouded with depression. Focusing on shortcomings in our character and failings in our dealings with people and work, for example, or the harm we may have done to others, we develop an unfair, low opinion of ourselves. This self-image becomes more and more concrete with time. We identify ourselves as incapable and inadequate and feel hopeless and depressed. Or we turn to other people in an attempt to find happiness and fulfillment. However, as our friends are likely to feel the same way about themselves, such relationships often bring only more frustration.

We can unlock the potential for happiness and satisfaction that lies within every one of us by becoming aware of our mental processes, and then applying discriminating wisdom to all our actions of body, speech, and mind. But to hope to be able to achieve this, and, through it, fulfillment, without first completing the necessary groundwork is to invite frustration. We must start by building a firm foundation, based on a realistic view of ourselves. We have to accept our positive as well as our negative traits, and determine to nourish the good and transform or eliminate the bad aspects of our character. Eventually we will recognize how fortunate we are to have been born human. Once we understand this, we can begin to train our minds to achieve enlightenment.

When we look at ourselves deeply, carefully, we find that most of our day-to-day problems are quite trivial. It is only our projections and conceptions that complicate them and allow them to grow out of all proportion. As we self-indulgently become caught up in our problems, they appear to grow larger and larger, and we disappear into deep states of depression and hopelessness. Wallowing in self-pity, we are unable to see that, in fact, we have created our problems and, therefore, our depressive state.

This meditation is an antidote to negative states of being such as depression and hopelessness. It helps us to recognize and rejoice in our good fortune, in our extraordinary and unique potential to achieve true happiness and satisfaction. An understanding of this potential naturally fills us with joy and enthusiasm for life—who wouldn't feel elated at the realization that they hold the key to their own fulfillment? At the same time, recognizing our good fortune helps us to see clearly that there are many who are infinitely less fortunate than we are. We feel true compassion for them and take an active concern in their plight.

The Practice

Sit comfortably with your back straight. Relax your body and let any tension dissolve and flow away.... Spend a few minutes calming and settling your mind using the meditation on the breath or the nine-round breathing practice.

Motivation

When your mind is calm and settled in the here-and-now, generate a positive, altruistic motivation for doing the meditation. You can think, for example, "May this meditation bring greater peace and happiness to myself and others, to the whole world," or "May this meditation bring me closer to enlightenment so that I can help all other beings attain enlightenment as well."

Begin the meditation by contemplating that the nature of your mind is clear and pure, and has the potential to become enlightened: the state of complete purity, goodness, and perfection. This is true for yourself and all other beings. You can think, for example, "The nature of every being's mind is clear like space, vast, and unlimited. Our negative thoughts and emotions are not permanent, fixed parts of the mind, but are transient, like clouds that pass through the sky. And because they are based on ignorance and misconceptions, they can be cleared away and the mind can be developed to a state that is completely pure and positive."

Alternatively, if you find it difficult to accept that the mind has the potential to become enlightened, you can think of the positive qualities that you have—intelligence, loving-kindness, compassion, generosity, courage, etc.—and remind yourself that these can be developed even further, and that you can use your life to bring benefit and happiness to others.

Spend some time contemplating this, and feel joyful about the potential that lies within you.

Although all beings have the potential to transform their mind and become enlightened, not all beings are in the most ideal situation in which they can recognize and develop this potential. Human beings are generally in the best situation. Non-human beings either have too much suffering or are incapable of developing their potential due to ignorance and other delusions.

Imagine what it would be like as an animal, for example. Animals in the wild have no one to care for them when they experience hunger, thirst, heat, cold, sickness, or injuries, and are in almost constant fear for their lives. Domestic animals are sometimes better off, but lack freedom and are often killed for meat, fur, or other products. And all animals, even the most intelligent, have extremely limited mental capacities and are unable to develop themselves intellectually or spiritually. Contemplate this to get a sense of how fortunate you are to have a human life.

However, not all human beings have the right conditions to recognize and develop their potential. Imagine, for example, being a destitute beggar, or living in a war zone. Most of your time and energy would be spent simply trying to keep yourself and your family alive; you would have little or no time to think of anything else such as spiritual practice.

Imagine suffering from a severe mental disability or illness, which would make it very difficult for you to understand the teachings on the mind's potential and how to develop it. Or having a physical condition that caused you a great deal of pain, discomfort, and inconvenience, and hindered your ability to learn and practice spiritual teachings.

Some people do not have access to spiritual teachings that explain the mind's potential and how to develop it. Imagine spending your entire life in a small, remote village where no one has even heard about enlightenment, so there's no opportunity to learn how to attain it.

Other people may be aware of their potential and sincerely wish to practice the teachings on how to develop it, but are prevented from doing so by others. For example, people in some countries do not have freedom of religion; others face strong objections from their parents, spouse, or children. Imagine yourself in such a situation, recognize how difficult it would be, and appreciate the freedom that you have.

Then, there are many people who are physically and mentally healthy, are materially well-off and have the freedom and opportunity to learn spiritual teachings, but are simply not interested. Their interests lie elsewhere: accumulating wealth, property, and possessions, acquiring worldly knowledge or skills, or in simply experiencing as much pleasure as they can. They never consider that all these things will be left behind when they die—like a dream that vanishes as soon as we wake up—and that only their mind will continue to the next life.

Some people engage in harmful actions such as killing, stealing, being abusive or dishonest, not realizing that these actions cause suffering to themselves and others, and create further obstacles to discovering their true potential. Recognize how fortunate you are to be interested in enlightenment and using your life in meaningful, beneficial ways, for yourself and others.

Now bring to mind the positive qualities and advantages you have. You are a human being with an intelligent mind, a loving heart, and a body you can put to good use. There are people who care about and support you—family, friends, a spiritual teacher. You have opportunities to pursue your creative, intellectual, and social interests. You enjoy a good standard of living—at least, you have enough to stay alive! And most of all, you have the potential and opportunity—because of all the other benefits—to investigate, understand, and transform your mind.

Even if your life does not afford as much freedom and comfort as you would like, and even if you have to live with some very difficult problems and challenges, no matter where you are and what conditions you live in, you can always work on your mind.

Think now how few people or creatures on earth share these freedoms and chances with you. When you have considered this deeply, you will realize how rare and precious a life like yours is. Really appreciate your good fortune.

Once you have seen the disadvantages your life is free of and the advantages you enjoy, decide how best to use your precious opportunities. Think of all the possibilities open to you—work, travel, enjoyment, study. If you wish to offer service to others, there are countless opportunities to help those less fortunate than you. But the most meaningful and beneficial thing you can do, both for yourself and others, is to develop yourself spiritually: overcoming the negative aspects of your mind and increasing the positive, and actualizing your potential for enlightenment.

Try to see the limitations of a lifestyle geared solely to materialistic gain. Think of the insignificance of fame, wealth, reputation, and sensual indulgence when compared to the goal of enlightenment. Why aspire to only temporal achievements when we are capable of so much more?

See if you can feel a sense of joy and appreciation for the wonderful situation you have. Resolve to use your life wisely—doing your best to avoid harming others, and instead helping them as much as you can, and developing your love, compassion, wisdom, and other positive qualities that will enable you to actualize your highest potential.

Finally, dedicate the energy and inspiration you have gained from doing this meditation to the ultimate happiness of all beings.

Common Problems in Meditation

Restlessness and Distraction

At times during a meditation session the mind is very restless and our attention is continually distracted by other things. These can include external objects like sounds, but also internal distractions such as memories of the past, fantasies about the future, or incessant chatter about what's happening in the present. Such thoughts are often accompanied by disturbing emotions, such as attachment (grasping at pleasant experiences); anger or hatred (obsessing over what some-one did that hurt or irritated us); fear; doubt; jealousy; or depression. Normally we just let the mind run like this without trying to con-trol it, so mental wandering has become a deeply ingrained habit.

It is not easy to give up habits, but we should recognize that this one—this mental excitement, as it's called—is the very opposite of meditation. As long as we are busy running in circles on the surface of the mind we will never penetrate to its depths and never develop the concentration we need for perceiving reality.

There are a number of methods for counteracting mental excite-ment. One is to focus firmly on the breath and let the mind become as calm and even as the natural rhythm of your breathing. Every time your attention wanders, bring it back to the breath. Observe what-ever thoughts and feelings arise without getting involved in them; recall that they are just waves of your mind, rising and falling.

An effective method from the Tibetan tradition for calming the mind is known as the nine-round breathing practice. This can be used at the beginning of a meditation session, or in the middle of a session, if your mind gets out of control:

1. For the first three breaths, breathe in through the right nostril and out through the left. If you wish, you can use your forefinger to close the left nostril while you breathe in and to close the right when you breathe out.

2. For the next three breaths, breathe in through the left nostril and out through the right. Again, you can use your forefinger to close the nostril you are not using.

3. For the last three breaths, breathe in through both nostrils and out through both.

With each breath, keep your mind focused on the breath and on the sensations you can feel at the nostrils as the breath goes in and out. Do not let your mind be distracted by thoughts or anything else. You can repeat the nine rounds several times if you wish, then return to your main meditation practice.

If mental restlessness is a recurring problem, check your posture. The spine should be very straight and the head tilted slightly forward with the chin tucked slightly in—the mind tends to be more restless when the head is raised too high. Reducing the amount of light in the room could also help, as bright light can stir up thoughts and feelings.

Patience is essential in dealing with a busy mind. Don't be upset with yourself if you can't keep your attention on the object of meditation. It takes time and persistent practice to learn to slow down and gain some control over the mind, so be easy on yourself.

Sleepiness and Dullness

The very opposite of excitement is sleepiness. This can vary from a dull, listless state of mind to near-unconsciousness. It is related to another of our habits: usually, when we close our eyes and relax our mind and body, it's time to go to sleep!

First, make sure that your back is straight and your head is not bent forward too far. Open your eyes halfway and meditate with your gaze directed at the floor in front of you. Increasing the amount of light in the room should also help you to stay alert.

Another solution is to visualize your mind enclosed within a tiny seed in the central channel at the level of your navel, as before. This time, imagine that the seed shoots up the central channel and out through the crown of your head. The seed opens and your mind merges with vast, empty space. Concentrate on this experience for a while, then return to the meditation.

If you continually struggle with sleepiness, it's often best to either take a break—you can splash cold water on your face, get some fresh air, or do some stretching—or stop the meditation altogether and try again later.

Physical Discomfort

Your meditations will flow smoothly if your body is relaxed and comfortable, but often it is difficult to get it into that state. Much of our physical tension is mind-related, arising from unresolved problems, fears, worries, or anger. The most effective solution is to recognize these problems and settle them in meditation. A short-term method for easing physical tension—to be used either at the beginning of a meditation session or during it—is to sweep the body with your attention. Start at the top of the head and travel downward through the body. Concentrate briefly on each part and consciously let it relax. Imagine that the tension simply dissolves.

Another method is to breathe deeply and slowly, and with much concentration imagine that the tension or pain leaves your body with each exhalation.

If neither of these methods works, you could try a more elaborate one: visualizing your body as hollow. Starting at the center of your chest, imagine that all the internal, solid parts of your body dissolve into light, and then into empty space. Everything within your chest, head, arms, and legs gradually dissolves and becomes empty. Your skin transforms into a very thin membrane of light to enclose this empty space. Concentrate for a while on this experience of your body being hollow, like a balloon.

If sitting causes discomfort or pain—in the knees or back, for example—it is all right to change to a more comfortable position. As meditation is an activity of the mind, not the body, it is more important to keep the mind clear and comfortable. However, at times it is useful just to observe the pain, which is a conscious experience, a mental perception, and try to overcome the usual fearful reaction to it. Instead of giving it the label "pain," see it as just a sensation, another type of energy. Doing such analysis should give you more insight into the workings of your mind and help you develop more control over your physical reactions.

An extension of this method of dealing with physical pain is mentally to increase it as much as possible. Imagine it getting worse and worse. After a while, return to the original pain—which now appears much less painful than before!

Another method is to visualize the suffering of all the beings of the universe and then, with great compassion, bring it mentally into the pain you are experiencing now. Think that you have taken on the pain of all beings, who are thus freed of all their suffering. Hold this thought and rejoice in it for as long as you can.

It is good to experiment with these methods for dealing with pain—but be careful not to overdo them and cause yourself an injury!

Noise

Although it is best to meditate in a quiet place, it's not always possible to find one. In the city we hear traffic, TVs and music, kids playing, people talking and yelling, airplanes passing overhead. But even out in the country or high in the mountains there are sounds: birds and animals, the wind blowing, a stream or river. It's unrealistic to think we can find a perfectly sound-free place to meditate, and it's mistaken to think that we can only meditate when there is no noise; rather it's a question of learning how to deal with it.

The problem is not so much the noise itself, but rather how our mind reacts to it. If the noise is pleasant, such as music we like, we feel attracted and want to pay attention to it rather than our object of meditation—that is attachment. If the noise is unpleasant, we feel irritation or aversion. Either way, we get stuck to the noise and it's difficult to let go of it and carry on with the meditation. Our mind starts making commentary about the noise: what it is, who's making it, recalling similar experiences in the past, thinking of trying to make it stop, and so on. It's these thoughts and feelings that are the problem.

The best way to deal with this situation is to recognize what is happening in your mind and learn to just be aware of the noise without reacting and making commentary on it. Realize that you can't stop the world from making noise just because you are meditating, but you can work on how your mind reacts. You might recall times when you were studying for an exam or engrossed in reading a really good book, and how you were oblivious to noise around you. You can learn to do the same while meditating.

Working on your mind is the best solution, but it's okay to try to stop or reduce the noise if that doesn't cause problems for anyone. You can also arrange your schedule so that you meditate when things are more quiet, such as early in the morning, or wear ear plugs!

Strange Images and Sensations

Meditators sometimes experience unusual images appearing in the mind, or sensations such as the body expanding or shrinking, or the mind floating outside the body. These are normal reactions as the mind adjusts itself to new activity and nothing to worry about.

On the other hand, do not be attached to such experiences or try to repeat them—this will only distract you from the real purpose of meditation. Simply observe whatever images or feelings arise without clinging to or rejecting them, and let them disappear of their own accord.

However, if any disturbing experience occurs frequently and you are unable to free yourself from it, you should consult a meditation teacher or a more experienced practitioner. It might be best to discontinue your practice until you receive someone's advice.

Discouragement

We often hear people complain, "I can't meditate; I've tried but it doesn't work," or "I've been meditating for so many months but nothing is happening." However, the problem is usually that they are expecting too much too quickly.

We need to be realistic. Most of us have never in our lives tried to understand our mind or control our thoughts and feelings. Old habits are not easy to break. Even if the results of daily meditation don't appear for two or three years—although this is highly unlikely—it should not be a cause for worry or despair.

Positive changes do not appear suddenly out of the blue, but develop slowly, gradually, little by little every day, so be patient with yourself. Remember, just making an effort to understand and control the mind is meditation. If you are trying to do what is best for yourself and others, you can feel confident that your meditation is worthwhile.

Often, new meditators think that their negative minds are getting worse, not better! And they feel that it is meditation that has caused this. Consider, however, what happens when you wash clothes. When you first put them into water, a certain amount of dirt comes out. As you continue to scrub them the water gets dirtier and dirtier. You might even be surprised by the amount of dirt that they contained. It would be foolish to blame the soap, water, and scrubbing for the dirt—the process of washing merely reveals what is there already, and is the right method for completely removing the dirt.

Similarly, meditation is the way to purify the mind of what is already there: at first we discover the gross negativities, then the more subtle ones.

So be patient and don't worry!

Recommended Reading

Buddhist Teachings on Death and Dying

Mind of Clear Light: Advice on Living Well and Dying Consciously by His Holiness the Dalai Lama and Jeffrey Hopkins. New York: Atria Books.

The Wheel of Death edited by Philip Kapleau. New York: Harper & Row.

Death, Intermediate State and Rebirth by Lati Rinpochay and Jeffrey Hopkins. Ithaca, NY: Snow Lion.

Path to Enlightenment in Tibetan Buddhism by Geshe Acharya Thubten Loden. Melbourne: Tushita Publications.

Death and Dying: The Tibetan Tradition by Glen H. Mullin. London: Arkana.

Liberation in the Palm of Your Hand, pp. 332–61, by Pabongka Rinpoche. Boston: Wisdom.

The Tibetan Book of Living and Dying by Sogyal Rinpoche. San Francisco: HarperCollins.

The Tibetan Book of the Dead translated by Robert A.F. Thurman. New York: Bantam Books.

The Great Treastise on the Stages of the Path to Enlightenment, Volume 1, Chapter 9, by Tsong-Kha-Pa. Ithaca, NY: Snow Lion.

Buddhist Meditation

How to Be Happy by Lama Zopa Rinpoche, edited by Josh Bartok and Ailsa Cameron. Boston: Wisdom.

Transforming Problems into Happiness by Lama Zopa Rinpoche, edited by Robina Courtin and Ailsa Cameron. Boston: Wisdom.

The Experience of Insight by Joseph Goldstein. Boston: Shambhala.

Mindfulness in Plain English by Bhante Henepola Gunaratana. Boston: Wisdom.

How to Meditate by Kathleen McDonald. Boston: Wisdom.

Lovingkindness: The Revolutionary Art of Happiness by Sharon Salzberg. Boston: Shambhala.

The Miracle of Mindfulness by Thich Nhat Hanh. Berkeley: Parallax Press.

Caring for the Dying

I Don't Know What to Say: How to Help and Support Someone Who Is Dying by Dr. Robert Buckman. London: Papermac.

Final Gifts: Understanding the Special Awareness, Needs and Communications of the Dying by Maggie Callanan and Patricia Kelley. New York: Bantam.

On Death and Dying by Elisabeth Kübler-Ross. New York: Collier.

Who Dies? An Investigation of Conscious Living and Conscious Dying by Stephen Levine. Garden City, NY: Doubleday.

Facing Death and Finding Hope by Christine Longaker. London: Century.

About the Authors

LAMA ZOPA RINPOCHE is one of the most internationally renowned masters of Tibetan Buddhism, working and teaching ceaselessly on almost every continent.

He is the spiritual director and co-founder of the Foundation for the Preservation of the Mahayana Tradition (FPMT), an international network of Buddhist projects, including monasteries in six countries and meditation centers in over thirty; health and nutrition clinics, and clinics specializing in the treatment of leprosy and polio; as well as hospices, schools, publishing activities, and prison outreach projects worldwide.

Lama Zopa Rinpoche is the author of numerous books, including *Transforming Problems into Happiness*, *Ultimate Healing*, and *How to Be Happy*.

KATHLEEN MCDONALD (Sangye Khadro) was born in California in 1952. She took her first courses in Buddhist meditation in Dharamsala, India, in 1973 and was ordained as a Tibetan Buddhist nun a year later. She lived with the community of Western monks and nuns at Kopan, the monastery of her teachers, Lama Thubten Yeshe and Lama Thubten Zopa Rinpoche, in Kathmandu, Nepal, where she studied and did meditation retreats.

In 1978 she moved to England to continue her higher Buddhist studies, and in 1982 helped establish the FPMT's Dorje Pamo

Monastery for Buddhist nuns in France. From 1985 until 1987 she taught in Australia, then for a year in Nepal, followed by eleven years as resident teacher at FPMT's Amitabha Buddhist Centre in Singapore. Since 2000 she has been teaching around the world, taking a break in mid-2005 for a year's solitary retreat in Spain.

To find out more about the FPMT, contact:

FPMT International Office
1632 SE 11th Avenue
Portland, OR 97214-4702 USA
Tel. (503) 808-1588 | Fax (503) 808-1589
www.fpmt.org

The Lama Yeshe Wisdom Archive

The Lama Yeshe Wisdom Archive (LYWA) houses an archival collection of the teachings of Lama Zopa Rinpoche and his teacher, Lama Thubten Yeshe. To find out more, contact:

LYWA
PO Box 356
Weston, MA 02493 USA
Tel. (781) 259-4466 | www.lamayeshe.com

Wisdom Publications

WISDOM PUBLICATIONS, a nonprofit publisher, is dedicated to making available authentic Buddhist works for the benefit of all. We publish translations of the sutras and tantras, commentaries and teachings of past and contemporary Buddhist masters, and original works by the world's leading Buddhist scholars. We publish our titles with the appreciation of Buddhism as a living philosophy and with the special commitment to preserve and transmit important works from all the major Buddhist traditions.

To learn more about Wisdom, or to browse books online, visit our website at wisdompubs.org. You may request a copy of our mail-order catalog online or by writing to this address:

Wisdom Publications
199 Elm Street
Somerville, Massachusetts 02144 USA
Telephone: (617) 776-7416
Fax: (617) 776-7841
Email: info@wisdompubs.org
www.wisdompubs.org

THE WISDOM TRUST

As a nonprofit publisher, Wisdom is dedicated to the publication of fine Dharma books for the benefit of all sentient beings and is dependent upon the kindness and generosity of sponsors in order to do so. If you would like to make a donation to Wisdom, please do so through our Somerville office. If you would like to sponsor the publication of a book, please write or email us at the address above.

Thank you.

Wisdom is a nonprofit, charitable 501(c)(3) organization affiliated with the Foundation for the Preservation of the Mahayana Tradition (FPMT).